SHEET PAN DINNERS

SHEET PAN DINNERS

Over 150 all-in-one dishes, including meat, fish, vegetarian and vegan recipes

JENNY TSCHIESCHE & LIZ FRANKLIN

Photography by Steve Painter

RYLAND PETERS & SMALL
LONDON • NEW YORK

Designer Paul Stradling
Desk Editor Emily Calder
Head of Production Patricia Harrington
Creative Director Leslie Harrington
Editorial Director Julia Charles

Photography & prop styling Steve Painter
Food stylist Lucy McKelvie

Indexer Vanessa Bird

First published in 2022 by
Ryland Peters & Small
20–21 Jockey's Fields,
London WC1R 4BW
and 341 E 116th St,
New York NY 10029

www.rylandpeters.com

10 9 8 7 6 5 4 3 2 1

NOTES

• Both British (Metric) and American (Imperial plus US cups) measurements are included in these recipes for your convenience; however it is important to work with one set of measurements only and not alternate between the two within a recipe.

• All spoon measurements are level unless otherwise specified. A teaspoon is 5 ml, a tablespoon is 15 ml.

• All eggs are medium (UK) or large (US), unless specified as large, in which case US extra-large should be used. Uncooked or partially cooked eggs should not be served to the very old, frail, young children, pregnant women or those with compromised immune systems.

• Ovens should be preheated to the specified temperatures. We recommend using an oven thermometer. If using a fan-assisted oven, adjust temperatures according to the manufacturer's instructions.

MIX
Paper from responsible sources
FSC® C106563
www.fsc.org

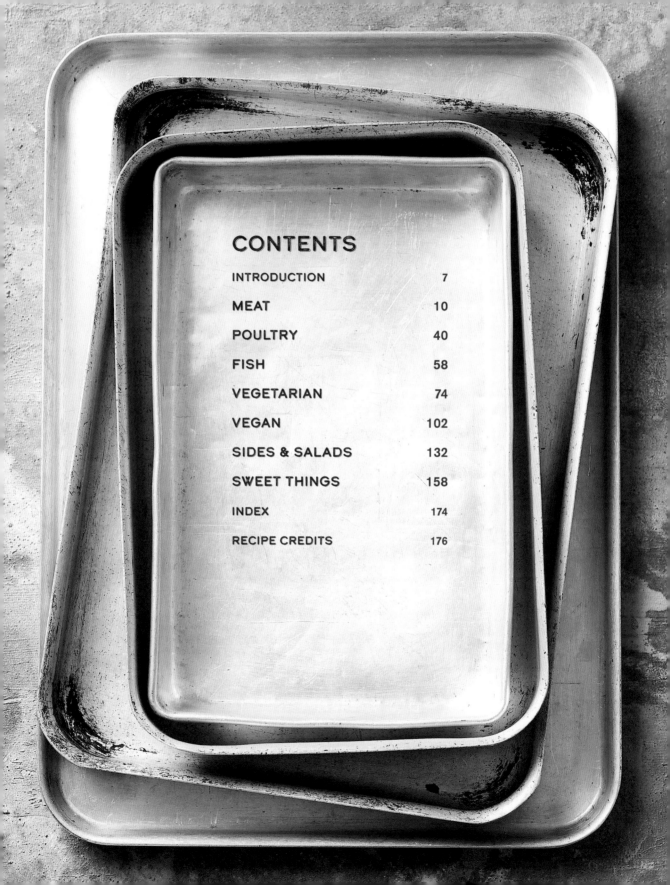

CONTENTS

INTRODUCTION 7

MEAT 10

POULTRY 40

FISH 58

VEGETARIAN 74

VEGAN 102

SIDES & SALADS 132

SWEET THINGS 158

INDEX 174

RECIPE CREDITS 176

INTRODUCTION

Modern life is busy, chaotic, and full on. Sometimes getting dinner on the table seems like the hardest thing to do after a long day, let alone trying to think up something nutritious everyone will like. It is surprising, therefore, that out of all the modern gadgets in our kitchens designed to make our lives easier, the greatest piece of equipment of them all turns out to be the simplest; the sheet pan, also known as the baking tray or roasting tin. As you will find out in this book, you barely need anything else, apart from a knife or two and (occasionally) a frying pan/skillet.

Above all, this book is for families, particularly those parents who want to ensure that the next generation grow up with a real food culture, not a processed food culture. I'm a nutritionist who works away from home, running workshops or in clinic, and this one pan way of cooking has, on so many occasions, saved me from the edge of madness. It's one of those methods that really requires very little thought and, importantly, little skill. While I am a recipe developer, I am not a chef so you won't find you're being expected to use any fancy culinary skills in this book. What you will find is simple recipes that are achievable by all.

I spent several years studying for a nutrition degree at the Institute of Optimum Nutrition while raising a family, and learnt the hard way that family life and healthy eating do not always go hand in hand. Once I graduated, I set about advising groups of parents, young athletes and those in the corporate environment on well-being and optimal nutrition through workshops and in my nutrition clinic. As time went by I realized that whilst theory is a good thing, practical advice is even better. The practical advice that spoke loudest and reaped the greatest benefits seemed to be in the form of simple recipes.

What started out as developing recipes for my workshops and clients grew in an unexpected direction. I was soon developing recipes for major health campaigns run by the BBC and Cancer Research to name a few as well as for many large brands of kitchenware. It's something I have developed a real passion for and simply love to do. I've worked in schools, for sports

organisations and individuals and one of the things that makes me most excited is working with families to make healthy eating easier, whether it is making lunchboxes more interesting or dinner times less stressful.

Each recipe or recipe combination in this book aims to present the opportunity to consume multiple vegetables as well as the right balance of other food groups. In particular I include the right kinds of fats, i.e. those our body knows how to break down and metabolize, and the right kinds of protein from identifiable sources and in an unadulterated and unprocessed (other than cheese, of course) form. The simplicity of a meal that combines some protein, some fat and some carbohydrate, is something our bodies will thank us for both now and in years to come. It's a way of eating we were designed to benefit from. Whilst some are lighter meals others are full-on family feasts, and some are even dinner-party worthy. I've also made suggestions regarding which recipes might work well alongside one another.

Way back when man discovered fire and the benefits provided by fire, the culinary possibilities exploded and we really started thriving and surviving as a species. Nowadays, we are not thriving so much, and you could argue we are not surviving either. More like hanging on by our fingernails. Some experts believe this current generation of children may not outlive their parents and that's largely due to the environment in which children are growing up. One of the issues with modern living is the abundance of processed junk food. This book aims to show you just how easy and how simple a step it is to take to create colourful, diverse tray bakes. These are the sorts of meals that the whole family will enjoy, making it possible to sit down together for a meal. If that's not a possibility due to your varied time schedules then simply leave some portions on low in the oven for later; or save the leftovers from the night before and serve these up the following day in lunchboxes or as an earlier evening meal for younger children.

One piece of advice is this; do not get stressed about providing foods that your children will eat every meal. Even when they do refuse to eat something remember that so long as they are exposed to that foodstuff regularly it won't become an issue. Just don't force them to eat it. With cooking on a sheet pan children can also get involved as it is such a simple method of cooking. Experience and scientific studies tell us that those who are involved in the process of creating a meal are far more likely to consume that meal too.

This book will show you that real food meals are not rocket science. They are not complicated and they don't take a huge amount of your time. It's about making the oven do the work. As you gain confidence with this method of cooking you'll find there are so many possibilities and with each you'll free up more of your valuable time. There's now no need to compromise.

Real food ingredients are the very basis of healthy eating. Creating recipes that combine real food ingredients in a nutritionally balanced way has been a pleasure and a joy. I hope that you too can gain from the simplicity of the recipes shared as part of this book.

STORECUPBOARD EXPLANATIONS

Stevia powder This is a natural sweetener that is known to have a glycaemic index of zero. What that means is that it doesn't raise your blood sugar levels when you eat it. However, when purchasing stevia powder be clear in what you are looking for. You want as pure as possible without added artificial sweeteners. Buying the powder in a pure form means you can use tiny amounts in place of larger amounts of sugar because it is so sweet. So for example, 200 g/1 cup sugar is equivalent to about ½ teaspoon stevia.

Coconut sugar This is a natural sugar made from the sap of the coconut tree. Unlike white, refined sugar, it is known to retain quite a few nutrients found in the coconut palm. The Philippine Department of Agriculture measured the glycaemic index of coconut sugar as 35. This is much lower than table sugar, which is somewhere around 65.

Garlic powder This is dehydrated ground garlic and it gives the flavour but not texture of fresh garlic to a dish.

Onion powder This is made from dehydrated onions that have been ground into a powder. Of course you will get great flavour from this condiment.

Mustard powder This is made from grinding mustard seeds. It's not as pungent as the jars of mustard we use with cooked meat. It's a fantastic flavour provider though, especially in marinades and burgers.

Tamari or coconut aminos Soy sauce is made to varying standards and sometimes with unwanted additives. Buying tamari, which is a gluten-free version of soy sauce, is often a good way to buy purer soy sauce. If you want a soy-free version, then coconut aminos are recommended.

Tempeh This is a fermented soy food. Fermented foods in general are very good for our gut health as they help to populate the gut with better bacteria.

Miso This is another fermented soy product that not only provides beneficial bacteria for the gut but also gives dishes a satisfying 'umami' taste.

Kefir/Greek yogurt Both kefir and good quality Greek yogurt contain probiotic bacteria which have been shown to improve the populations of good bacteria in the gut. This in turn can provide a boost to the immune system. Kefir can be purchased from health food stores or Polish supermarkets.

Coconut milk yogurt For those who want a creamy, dairy-free alternative to yogurt, there's a range of non-dairy coconut milk-based yogurts now on the market.

Ghee This is butter that has had the moisture, proteins and sugars removed. It therefore doesn't burn. It's also a source of Vitamins A, D and K2 fats.

Coconut oil The structure of coconut oil, being primarily Medium Chain Triglycerides (other saturated fats are mostly Long Chain), means it is very easily digested. It requires very little bile and few digestive enzymes to break down coconut oil.

Balsamic glaze This glaze should be made from a combination of cooked grape must and balsamic vinegar, which creates a mellower and less tart flavour than balsamic vinegar on its own.

Plantains Although part of the banana family they do need cooking before eating. Ripe plantain is used in a variety of dishes, both savoury and sweet. In this book

I've used fried plantain chips as a gluten-free crispy coating for chicken nuggets.

EQUIPMENT EXPLANATIONS

Baking multiple whole meals on sheet pans calls for at least two different-sized pans. In the course of writing this book I have trialled a lot of different sheet pans. I would say my favourites have been stoneware, stainless steel or silicone for ease of use and taste reasons. I am sure you will have an inclination about which you might prefer, but if you don't and are just starting out, the stainless steel is probably the most cost-effective place to start.

The sizes I tend to use are a small dish, such as a loaf pan, 450 g/1 lb. or 900 g/2 lb. in capacity, a 20 x 20 cm/ 8 x 8 in. sheet pan and a large roasting pan. Of course some implements such as spatulas, fish slices and wooden spoons have also been essential, as have adjustable measuring spoons to help get the balance of spices, herbs and other additions right.

I love having a food processor handy for making dishes even more quickly, especially sauces for some of the saucier tray bakes. Being able to finely chop onions, garlic and herbs, for example, in a food processor makes the whole process that much less hassle. That doesn't mean you have to make a large investment (or any at all if you are handy with a knife and can cut things fine, unlike me) as even a manual food processor can help speed things up a little.

This book will open up a range of possibilities as far as roasting vegetables go, and to that end will make some vegetables far more appealing to some, let's say limited palates, than they have been previously.

WHAT VEGETABLES TO ROAST?

When you mention 'roast vegetables' to people they tend to respond with 'oh yes, we love roasted Mediterranean veg in our household' or indeed 'we love roast potatoes with our Sunday lunch'. However, you can roast so many more vegetables than either of these two common examples allow for. If you're not sure if a particular vegetable can be roasted, my recommendation is to just give it a try. It might not end up being your favourite way to eat that vegetable, but it's definitely worth the experiment to find out.

A Good dose of good fat Toss your chopped vegetables in sufficient oil to coat evenly. Ideal oils include olive oils, ghee, butter (melted) or coconut oil. One sheet pan may need 1–2 tablespoons oil/fat. The exception to this is aubergine/eggplant where you'll need up to 3 tablespoons oil for a large aubergine/eggplant because they absorb so much of the oil, but then that's part of their appeal. The oil/fat greatly improves the cooking and flavour.

Add some seasoning Most vegetables benefit from the addition of sea salt and often some pepper too. You can also add other flavoursome seasoning such as vinegar, spices and herbs to really make the flavours come alive.

Choose the sheet pan carefully In order that the vegetables cook evenly there should be a bit of space in the pan you're baking them in. For this reason it's good to have more than one sheet pan available to you at any one time. If the vegetables are too crowded they tend to steam rather than bake. That's not the texture nor the taste that you're looking for.

Preheat the oven Make sure your oven is hot before you put the vegetables in. I like to roast my vegetables at 200°C (400°F) Gas 6. There are exceptions to this. For example roasted potatoes are better and crispier at hotter temperatures.

When are they cooked? The cooked vegetables should be tender when a fork is poked into them. They may also be some charred bits on the edges.

General roasting times for vegetables Cooking times are for roasting vegetables at 200°C (400°F) Gas 6.
Root vegetables: 35–45 minutes, depending on how small you cut them.
Cruciferous vegetables: 15–25 minutes, depending on how small you cut them.
Green Vegetables and Nightshades: 10–30 minutes, depending on how you cut them.
Onions: 30–45 minutes, depending on how crispy you like them and how you cut them.

MEAT

ALL-IN-ONE BREAKFAST

You'll need just five ingredients for this simple one pan dish. It's a delicious twist on the traditional breakfast of bacon and eggs and so quick to prepare you'll make it all the time.

4 large field mushrooms
2 tablespoons olive oil
12 slices Parma ham/prosciutto or bresaola
4 eggs
1 tablespoon freshly chopped parsley
sea salt and freshly ground black pepper

SERVES 2

Preheat the oven to 220°C (425°F) Gas 7.

Place the mushrooms on a sheet pan with sides. Drizzle over the olive oil and season with salt and pepper.

Bake in the preheated oven for 15 minutes. Check that the mushrooms are almost cooked through. If not, cook for up to a further 5 minutes.

Add the ham or bresaola to the sheet pan and crack the eggs on top.

Bake for another 7–10 minutes until the eggs are just cooked.

Remove from the oven, sprinkle over the fresh parsley and enjoy.

BREAKFAST SLICE

Who says breakfast food even exists? There are cultures where there is no such thing as breakfast food. Food is food and can be eaten at any meal. We often consider eggs to be predominantly a breakfast food so I've named this Breakfast Slice, but honestly, you could enjoy it any time of day.

6 eggs
2 medium courgettes/zucchini, grated
2 medium carrots, grated
2 onions, grated
5 slices unsmoked back bacon,
   finely chopped
1½ teaspoons dried mixed herbs
55 g/¼ cup ghee, plus a little more
   for greasing the pan
55 g/⅓ cup coconut flour
½ teaspoon sea salt
pinch of freshly ground black pepper

20 x 25-cm/8 x 10-in. sheet pan
   with sides, greased

SERVES 2-3

Preheat the oven to 200°C (400°F) Gas 6.

Whisk the eggs in a bowl until they are light and fluffy.

In a large bowl, mix together the eggs, grated vegetables, bacon, herbs, ghee, flour and seasoning.

Pour the mixture into the prepared sheet pan. Bake in the preheated oven for 45 minutes or until the top is golden brown and a fork inserted into the middle comes out clean. Serve immediately.

Serving Suggestion: Serve with baked mushrooms and sliced avocado.

BAKED EGGS WITH CHORIZO, TOMATO & SPINACH

A delicious mix of spicy chorizo and tangy tomatoes, combined with protein-rich eggs.
A feast for the eyes, full of naturally colourful ingredients, this will be a filling dinner winner!

160 g/5¾ oz. frozen spinach (defrosted,
    excess liquid removed by squeezing
    through a sieve/strainer and roughly torn)
4 tablespoons chorizo sausage,
    roughly chopped
300 g/10½ oz. passata/strained tomatoes
¾ teaspoon sea salt
4 eggs
a handful of fresh baby spinach leaves
    (optional)

SERVES 2

Preheat the oven to 220°C (425°F) Gas 7.

Place the spinach, chorizo and passata/strained tomatoes
in a small sheet pan with sides with the salt and stir to combine.
Make four small wells in the mixture and break in the eggs.

Bake in the preheated oven for 25 minutes or until the egg
whites are cooked. Serve immediately.

Serving Suggestion: Add fresh baby spinach leaves just
before serving to wilt gently over the dish.

SWEET POTATO & KALE HASH WITH BAKED EGGS

Bacon and eggs combine with the 'powerhouse' flavours of sun-dried tomatoes and sweet
potato and the super green leafy vegetable, kale, to create a delicious hash.

2 medium sweet potatoes
    (approx. 500 g/1 lb. 2 oz.),
    peeled and grated
65 g/¾ cup baby kale leaves
    or the same amount of kale,
    destalked and chopped
6 slices unsmoked back bacon,
    thinly sliced

1½ tablespoons dried oregano
90 g/½ cup sun-dried
    tomato pesto or sun-
    dried tomato paste
1 tablespoon olive oil
6 eggs

SERVES 2-4

Preheat the oven to 200°C (400°F) Gas 6.

Mix the sweet potato with the kale,
bacon, oregano, pesto/paste and olive
oil. Place the mixture into a sheet pan
with sides and bake in the preheated
oven for 15 minutes.

Make six holes in the mixture and then
crack in the eggs. Bake for a further
7–10 minutes until the eggs are just
cooked. Serve.

HONEY & MUSTARD SAUSAGE BAKE

Ah, honey and mustard, a classic flavour combination and one we have loved for years as a family. When I knew I would be creating an oven-based recipe book this combination with sausages immediately came to mind. This dish is one of those classics that gets made again and again and again.

3 red onions, cut into
   thin wedges
3 medium sweet potatoes,
   peeled and cut lengthways,
   then into 1-cm/½-in.
   semi-circles
300 g/10½ oz. asparagus,
   washed and trimmed
10 chestnut mushrooms,
   wiped clean

2 tablespoons olive oil
1 teaspoon sea salt
2 tablespoons wholegrain
   mustard
2 tablespoons honey
24 chipolatas

SERVES 6

Preheat the oven to 200°C (400°F) Gas 6.

Combine the vegetables in a large sheet pan with sides with the olive oil and salt and bake in the preheated oven for 10 minutes.

Meanwhile, combine the mustard and honey in a large bowl and stir in the sausages, leaving them to marinate for 10 minutes or so.

Add the sausages and the marinade to the sheet pan and give everything a good stir.

Bake for a further 25 minutes until the sausages are cooked through. Serve.

PORK MEATBALLS WITH SPROUTS & SWEET POTATO

Brussels sprouts – love them or hate them? Hopefully this combination will persuade you that they really are a welcome addition to some dishes. Trust me!

1 large onion, finely chopped
2 teaspoons garlic salt
1 kg/2¼ lb. minced/ground pork
½ teaspoon ground mace
½ teaspoon dried thyme
⅛ teaspoon white pepper
500 g/1 lb. 2 oz. Brussels
   sprouts, trimmed

3 small sweet potatoes
   (approx. 500 g/1 lb. 2 oz.
   peeled weight), peeled and
   cut into 2-cm/¾-in. cubes
4 tablespoons olive oil
½ teaspoon sea salt
3 garlic cloves, crushed
fresh thyme, to serve

SERVES 4

Preheat the oven to 200°C (400°F) Gas 6.

In a large bowl, mix together the onion, garlic salt, pork, ground mace, dried thyme and white pepper. Roll into table tennis-sized meatballs. Set aside.

Toss the sprouts and sweet potatoes in the olive oil, sprinkle over the salt and stir in the crushed garlic.

Put the vegetables on a large sheet pan with sides and bake in the preheated oven for 20 minutes.

Add the meatballs to the sheet pan, then bake for a further 25 minutes until the meatballs are cooked through. Serve with fresh thyme leaves scattered over the dish.

SAUSAGE, CELERY & TOMATO BAKE

Clean-tasting celery and the sharp and sweet flavours of the tomatoes combine brilliantly
with the salty sausages.

4 celery stalks, thickly sliced
  on the diagonal about
  2 cm/¾ in. each in length
1 red onion, quartered
2 garlic cloves, peeled
½ teaspoon sea salt
½ teaspoon freshly ground
  black pepper

1 tablespoon olive oil
4 large tomatoes (not beef
  tomatoes), cut into quarters
1 teaspoon fennel seeds
10 thick good-quality sausages

SERVES 4

Preheat the oven to 200°C (400°F) Gas 6.

In a large bowl, mix together the celery, onion, garlic, salt,
pepper and olive oil. Put the vegetables on a sheet pan
with sides and lay the tomato quarters on the outside
edges of the pan. Sprinkle over the fennel seeds. Lay the
sausages on top of the vegetables but not the tomatoes.

Bake in the preheated oven for 55 minutes. Turn the
sausages and the vegetables once during baking. Serve.

Serving Suggestion: Serve with baked sweet potatoes.

JERK PINEAPPLE PORK LOIN

Pork and pineapple go together so well. This is taste of the Caribbean in a dish.
It tastes great accompanied by coleslaw.

1¼ teaspoons sea salt
2 tablespoons jerk seasoning
500-g/1 lb. 2 oz. pork fillet
227-g/8-oz. can pineapple rings, drained
  (keep the juice)
300 g/10½ oz. new potatoes, chopped into
  1-cm/½-in. pieces
1 teaspoon olive oil
100 g/3½ oz. white cabbage, thickly sliced
1 tablespoon ghee or coconut oil

SERVES 4

Mix 1 teaspoon salt and the jerk seasoning together in a bowl. Cut the pork
fillet in half and roll each half in the salt/spice mix. Drizzle a tablespoon
of pineapple juice over each half fillet, cover and leave in the refrigerator
to marinate for 5–8 hours ideally.

When you're ready to cook, preheat the oven to 200°C (400°F) Gas 6.

Put the potatoes on a sheet pan with sides. Add the cabbage to the sheet
pan, then drizzle over the olive oil and sprinkle over the salt.

Heat the ghee or coconut oil in a frying pan/skillet. Add the pork fillets and
sear each side briefly. Wrap each half fillet in foil and place on the same sheet
pan as the potatoes. Bake in the preheated oven for 25 minutes until cooked.

Slice the pork and return to the pan. Pour any juices from their foil packages
into the pan. Stir the slices with the vegetables plus another 2 tablespoons
of the pineapple juice. Place back into the oven for just 1 minute to heat the
sauce through. Serve with a pineapple ring on each plate.

CROWD-PLEASER MEATLOAF & GARLIC BROCCOLI

What's not to love about a meatloaf? This one can certainly feed a family!
It's packed full of hidden vegetables too. That's a win-win!

8 slices unsmoked back bacon
2 carrots, roughly chopped
2 celery stalks, roughly chopped
1 onion, roughly chopped
2 garlic cloves, peeled
3 tablespoons freshly chopped parsley
800 g/1¾ lb. minced/ground beef
2 eggs
40 g/⅓ cup ground flaxseeds/linseeds
65 ml/¼ cup milk
1½ tablespoons butter/ghee/coconut oil
2 teaspoons sea salt
½ teaspoon freshly ground black pepper
1 head of broccoli, cut into florets
2 medium courgettes/zucchini, cut into
    2-cm/¾-in. slices
1 teaspoon garlic salt
2 teaspoons olive oil
3 tablespoons BBQ Sauce (no added sugar),
    such as Dr Will's, or balsamic glaze

33 x 22 x 10-cm/13 x 8½ x 4-in. loaf pan

SERVES 4-6

Preheat the oven to 200°C (400°F) Gas 6.

Lay four slices of the bacon in the base
of the loaf pan.

Put the carrots, celery, onion, garlic and
parsley in a food processor and finely chop.
Remove from the food processor and put
in a bowl. Mix in the minced/ground beef,
eggs, flaxseeds/linseeds, milk and butter/
ghee/coconut oil as well as the seasoning
until thoroughly combined.

Push the meat mixture into the loaf pan
on top of the bacon and top the mixture
with the remaining bacon slices, tucking
the ends down the sides of the loaf pan.

Bake in the preheated oven for 25 minutes.

Meanwhile, put the remaining prepared
vegetables onto a sheet pan with high
sides, sprinkle over the garlic salt and
drizzle over the olive oil.

Once 25 minutes is up, coat the top
of the meatloaf with the BBQ sauce
or balsamic glaze.

At this stage, put the vegetables into the
oven and bake both the meatloaf and the
vegetables for a further 25 minutes. Toss
the vegetables once during cooking.

Serve the meatloaf and the baked
vegetables together.

BEEF & CHORIZO MEATBALLS IN MEDITERRANEAN SAUCE WITH PEPPERS

Moist Spanish meatballs made from beef and chorizo combine with sweet peppers to create a scrumptious all-in-one meal.

1 medium red (bell) pepper, deseeded and cut into 1-cm/½-in. strips
1 medium orange (bell) pepper, deseeded and cut into 1-cm/½-in. strips
½ teaspoon sea salt
2 teaspoons olive oil
1 onion, finely chopped
1 garlic clove, finely chopped
500 g/1 lb. 2 oz. passata/ strained tomatoes
1 teaspoon dried marjoram or oregano
1 tablespoon tomato purée/paste
1 teaspoon garlic salt
½ teaspoon honey
100 g/3½ oz. chorizo
400 g/14 oz. minced/ ground beef

SERVES 4

Preheat the oven to 200°C (400°F) Gas 6.

Put the (bell) peppers on a sheet pan with high sides, sprinkle over the salt and drizzle over the olive oil. Bake in the preheated oven for 15 minutes.

Meanwhile, put the onion, garlic, passata/strained tomatoes, marjoram/oregano, tomato purée/paste, garlic salt and honey in a bowl and stir together to make a sauce.

To make the meatballs, finely chop the chorizo or use a food processor to grind it to a paste and mix it together with the minced/ground beef. Roll the minced meat mix into 12 evenly-sized meatballs.

After 15 minutes of cooking the (bell) peppers, add the sauce and the meatballs to the sheet pan. Cover with foil and bake for a further 25–30 minutes until the meatballs are just cooked and still moist. Serve.

ROOT VEG & CORNED BEEF HASH

The taste of my 1980s childhood but with a healthier twist. Still the familiar taste of corned beef, but now combined with root vegetables in place of the traditional potatoes, giving this a boost of nutrients.

500 g/1 lb. 2 oz. mixed root vegetables, coarsely chopped in a food processor (to about 1-cm/⅜-in. pieces)
3 small red onions, quartered
1 tablespoon Worcestershire sauce
1 teaspoon wholegrain mustard
1 tablespoon freshly chopped mixed herbs
3 tablespoons coconut oil or ghee
4 eggs
1 x 340-g/12-oz. can reduced-salt corned beef, cut into 2-cm/1-in. cubes

SERVES 4

Preheat the oven to 200°C (400°F) Gas 6.

In a large bowl, mix together the vegetables, Worcestershire sauce, mustard, herbs and coconut oil or ghee.

Spread the coated vegetables out on a sheet pan with sides. Bake in the preheated oven for 25 minutes.

Remove from the oven, make four wells in the vegetables and crack in the eggs. Add the corned beef and bake for a further 6–9 minutes or until the eggs are cooked. Serve immediately.

STEAK BURGERS WITH BALSAMIC ROAST VEGETABLES

OK, this is a bit of a cheat meal because someone has already made the steak burgers for you, but this quick-win midweek meal will be very well received.

2 onions, cut into eighths
2 courgettes/zucchini, cut into 2-cm/¾-in. thick semi-circles
6–8 mushrooms, cut into quarters
1 head of broccoli, cut into florets
2 tablespoons olive oil
1½ tablespoons balsamic glaze
¾ teaspoon sea salt
8 steak burgers

SERVES 4

Preheat the oven to 200°C (400°F) Gas 6.

In a large bowl, mix the vegetables, olive oil, balsamic glaze and salt together.

Put the vegetables on a sheet pan with sides and the steak burgers on a separate sheet pan. Bake both sheet pans in the preheated oven for 25 minutes or until both the vegetables and burgers are cooked. Serve.

Serving Suggestion: Add a dash of chilli/hot red pepper sauce for some heat.

ROASTED ROQUEFORT BURGERS WITH GARLIC BROCCOLI

The key to making these burgers moist and succulent is ensuring they're moulded into flat patties and getting the cooking time right. If you are not keen on blue cheese simply add your favourite cheese topping or go without the cheese. These burgers work well with crispy cooked broccoli.

800 g/1¾ lb. minced/ground beef
1 teaspoon sea salt
1 teaspoon dried thyme
1 teaspoon mustard powder
1 egg
2 teaspoons Worcestershire sauce
½ teaspoon freshly ground black pepper
1 large head of broccoli, cut into very small florets
1 tablespoon olive oil
½ teaspoon garlic salt
1 x vine of cherry tomatoes (with about 12 cherry tomatoes on the vine)
40 g/⅓ cup Roquefort cheese, crumbled

SERVES 4

Preheat the oven to 200°C (400°F) Gas 6.

In a large bowl, mix together the beef, salt, thyme, mustard powder, egg, Worcestershire sauce and pepper. Mix really well with your hands to ensure all of the seasonings are evenly distributed. Shape the mixture into eight equal burgers. Press the burgers flat to ensure even baking.

Put the broccoli on a sheet pan with sides and sprinkle over the olive oil and garlic salt. Lay the burgers on a wire rack in the preheated oven with another sheet pan below to catch the fat as it drips through.

Bake the burgers and the broccoli in the preheated oven for about 15–17 minutes. Turn the burgers after 5 minutes baking time. Add the vine tomatoes to the broccoli sheet pan 10 minutes before the end of cooking.

Once cooked, crumble the Roquefort over each burger. Serve the burgers, broccoli and tomatoes together.

SPICY ROAST BEEF WITH BUTTERNUT SQUASH & CABBAGE

A spicy marinade really brings pizzazz to this roast beef. Ideally, this should be served on the rare side for optimal flavour and texture. The butternut squash and cabbage really soak up the flavours in this one too.

850-g/1 lb. 14 oz. beef roasting joint
300 g/10½ oz. butternut squash, peeled, deseeded and cut into 2-cm/¾-in. pieces
200 g/7 oz. pointed cabbage, sliced

for the marinade
2 teaspoons sea salt
1 teaspoon coconut sugar
1 teaspoon smoked paprika
1 teaspoon garlic powder
1 teaspoon mustard powder
¾ teaspoon dried marjoram or oregano
¼ teaspoon freshly ground black pepper
2 tablespoons olive oil

SERVES 6

First combine the marinade ingredients in a small bowl or ramekin.

Place the beef on a sheet pan with sides large enough to fit the beef and the vegetables in. Rub the marinade all over the beef then cover with foil and leave to marinate for 1 hour at room temperature.

Preheat the oven to 200°C (400°F) Gas 6.

When the hour is up, add the butternut squash to the pan and roast both the beef and the squash together in the preheated oven for 1 hour 10 minutes, still covered in the foil to start with.

Add the cabbage with 30 minutes cooking time left to go and remove the foil. Give everything a good stir at the same time.

When the cooking is done, turn the oven off and take the beef joint out of the oven, then leave it to rest covered in foil, whilst the vegetables rest in the residual heat of the oven.

Once the beef has rested for 10 minutes, slice it thinly and serve with the vegetables.

BEEF-STUFFED TOMATOES

Actually, it was my father who asked for me to recreate these 'tomate farcie' as we first knew them. A summer holiday back in 1989 to the Alps, where this dish was so in season and we ate far too many of them, was his inspiration. Fast forward nearly 30 years and he suddenly took a fancy for them when he knew I was writing this book.

8 large tomatoes (not beef tomatoes)
250 g/9 oz. minced/ground beef
25 g/½ cup dried breadcrumbs or finely
  ground cornflakes
25 g/¼ cup ground almonds
½ onion, roughly chopped
2 tablespoons freshly chopped flat
  leaf parsley
1 tablespoon freshly chopped thyme leaves
40 g/⅓ cup Gruyère cheese, grated
½ teaspoon sea salt
1 tablespoon olive oil
sea salt and freshly ground black pepper

SERVES 4

Preheat the oven to 200°C (400°F) Gas 6.

Cut the tops off the tomatoes, but reserve the tops. Remove the seeds and flesh of the tomatoes using a serrated edged spoon or a combination of knife and spoon, being careful not to slice the tomatoes.

In a large bowl, mix together the minced/ground beef, breadcrumbs or cornflakes, ground almonds, onion, herbs, grated cheese and ½ teaspoon salt. Mix this really well, ideally by using your hands.

Put the empty tomatoes on a sheet pan with sides. Stuff each one with some of the beef mixture. Put the tomato lids back onto the tomatoes, drizzle with olive oil and sprinkle with salt and pepper. Bake in the preheated oven for 30 minutes until the tomatoes are soft and the beef mixture inside is cooked through. Serve.

Serving Suggestion: Serve with Twice Baked Cheesy Potatoes (page 135) and a green salad.

STEAK & CHIPS

2 minute steaks
2 sweet potatoes, peeled and cut
  into 1-cm/½-in. chips/fries
1 teaspoon extra virgin olive oil
½ teaspoon sea salt
10 cherry tomatoes, halved

for the marinade
2 teaspoons balsamic glaze
2 tablespoons olive oil
¼ teaspoon Dijon mustard
¼ teaspoon garlic salt
¼ teaspoon sea salt

SERVES 2

The key to a quick steak, especially a lower cost minute steak, is the marinade and the length of time the marinade is left on in advance of cooking. This steak dish needs a little advanced planning but not a lot, and is quick and simple as well as being a low cost and healthier way to enjoy steak and 'chips'/'fries'.

For the marinade, mix all of the ingredients together in a bowl or shake in a bottle to combine. Put the steaks in a flat bowl, cover with the marinade and leave to marinate in the refrigerator for 8–12 hours, uncovered, turning a couple of times.

When you're ready to cook, remove the steaks from the refrigerator. Preheat the oven to 200°C (400°F) Gas 6.

Toss the sweet potato chips/fries on a sheet pan with the olive oil and salt. Bake in the preheated oven or 15–20 minutes until cooked. Remove from the pan.

Add the steaks and cherry tomato halves to the sheet pan. Preheat the grill/broiler to high. Grill/broil the steaks for 2 minutes on one side and 1 minute on the other. Serve the steaks with the sweet potato chips/fries and tomatoes.

SMOKY LAMB RIBS WITH SLOW-ROASTED CARROTS

1 teaspoon coconut sugar
½ teaspoon smoked paprika
½ teaspoon mustard powder
½ teaspoon garlic powder
½ teaspoon onion powder
¼ teaspoon chilli/chili powder
¼ teaspoon sea salt
1 teaspoon dried oregano
1 teaspoon apple cider vinegar
2 tablespoons olive oil
4 large carrots, cut into 5-cm/2-in. batons
600 g/1 lb. 5 oz. lamb ribs

SERVES 2-3

Such a cost-effective cut of meat and so underrated. Discover how crowd-pleasing flavoursome lamb ribs can be with this recipe and keep your weekly food bill within budget at the same time.

Preheat the oven to 140°C (275°F) Gas 1.

In a small bowl, mix together the sugar, paprika, mustard powder, garlic powder, onion powder, chilli/chili powder, salt, oregano, vinegar and olive oil.

Put the carrot batons on a sheet pan with sides and put the lamb ribs on top of the carrots. Rub the spice mix all over the ribs.

Bake in the preheated oven for 1 hour, then reduce the temperature to 120°C (250°F) Gas ½ and cover tightly with foil. Bake for a further 1½ hours. Serve.

Serving Suggestion: Serve with Perfect Roast Potatoes (page 135).

MINTY LAMB BURGERS & VEG

Mint and lamb make an ideal partnership, and one that continues to work in these moist burgers. It's a very satisfying spring dish.

500 g/1 lb. 2 oz. minced/ground lamb
2 shallots, finely diced
1 garlic clove, crushed
10 g/⅓ cup freshly chopped mint
½ teaspoon ground cumin
1 teaspoon sea salt
2 medium sweet potatoes, peeled and cut into 3 x 1-cm/1¼ x ½-in. chips/fries
½ cauliflower, chopped into florets
1 teaspoon olive oil

SERVES 4

Preheat the oven to 200°C (400°F) Gas 6.

In a large bowl, mix together the minced/ground lamb, shallots, garlic, mint, cumin and ½ teaspoon of the salt thoroughly. Using your hands, form into four large, flat lamb burgers.

Place the sweet potato chips/fries and cauliflower florets on a sheet pan with sides. Drizzle over the olive oil and sprinkle over the remaining salt.

Bake in the preheated oven for 20 minutes. Then add the burgers to the pan and bake for a further 15 minutes. Check the burgers are cooked through. Serve immediately.

LAMB SKEWERS WITH ROASTED VEG

Lamb provides great flavour and works wonderfully well in baked recipes especially, as in this dish, with the complementary flavours of honey, garlic, tomato and tamari.

2 garlic cloves, thinly sliced
2 tablespoons tamari
2 tablespoons tomato
    purée/paste
1 tablespoon honey
5 sprigs of fresh thyme
800 g/1¾ lb. lamb steak, cut
    into 2-cm/¾-in. cubes
3 large carrots, sliced thickly
    on the diagonal about
    2-cm/¾-in. thick

2 tablespoons olive oil
2 medium red onions, quartered
2 medium courgettes/zucchini,
    sliced lengthways, then cut
    into semi-circles, about
    2-cm/¾-in. thick
200 g/7 oz. button mushrooms
sea salt

4 metal skewers

SERVES 4

Preheat the oven to 200°C (400°F) Gas 6.

To make the marinade, mix together the garlic, tamari, tomato purée/paste, honey and the leaves from 2 sprigs of thyme.

Mix the meat with the marinade and leave to marinate whilst preparing and cooking the vegetables.

Put the carrots onto a sheet pan with sides, drizzle over some of the olive oil and add a good pinch of salt and place in the preheated oven. After 10 minutes, add the onions, courgettes/zucchini, mushrooms and the remaining thyme to the pan. Drizzle with the remaining olive oil and a little more salt and bake for a further 15 minutes.

Meanwhile, thread the meat onto four metal skewers. Add these to the sheet pan containing the vegetables. Bake for a further 10 minutes until the meat is just cooked but still tender and all the veg are cooked and ready to eat. Serve.

LAMB KOFTA MEATBALLS & FRAGRANT SWEET POTATO WEDGES

These kofta meatballs are a family favourite of ours. We love them in different forms, whether they're cooked at a family BBQ, a meatball stew, or, as here, simply baked meatballs.

for the meatballs
800 g/1¾ lb. minced/ground lamb
¼ teaspoon ground turmeric
½ teaspoon ground cumin
1 teaspoon garlic granules
1 teaspoon onion powder
1 teaspoon sea salt
1 red onion, finely chopped
2 large garlic cloves, minced
20 g/⅓ cup freshly chopped
    coriander/cilantro
1 tablespoon honey

for the wedges
1 kg/2¼ lb. sweet potatoes,
    cut into wedges
1 teaspoon ground cumin
1 teaspoon black onion seeds
½ teaspoon sea salt
1 teaspoon olive oil, ghee
    or melted coconut oil

SERVES 4

Preheat the oven to 200°C (400°F) Gas 6.

For the wedges, put the sweet potato wedges in a bowl and add the cumin, black onion seeds, salt and olive oil, ghee or coconut oil and mix together. Put the wedges onto a non-stick sheet pan with sides, well-spaced apart, and bake in the preheated oven for 25 minutes, tossing once during cooking.

Meanwhile, make the meatballs. In a large bowl, mix together all the meatball ingredients by hand. Roll into small balls (about 20–25 in total) and, after 25 minutes cooking, place on the same sheet pan as the sweet potato wedges.

Bake in the oven for a further 15 minutes until cooked through. Serve the meatballs with the wedges.

MARINATED LAMB CHOPS WITH GARLICKY TOMATOES & WHITE BEANS

This is a summery dish that requires a little marinating time but is worth the wait. Using relatively few ingredients, you can create a really delicious meal.

8 lamb chops
7 plum tomatoes
3 garlic cloves, peeled
1 x 400-g/14-oz. can cannellini
    or white kidney beans
    (drained and rinsed)
2 tablespoons freshly chopped
    basil
1 teaspoon olive oil
½ teaspoon sea salt
freshly ground black pepper

for the marinade
75 ml/scant ⅓ cup olive oil
40 ml/3 tablespoons red wine
    vinegar
1 teaspoon sea salt

SERVES 4

In a shallow bowl (large enough for all the lamb chops), whisk the marinade ingredients together. Put the lamb chops in the bowl, turn to coat, then cover with foil and marinate in the refrigerator for 2 hours. Remove from the refrigerator 30 minutes before cooking.

Preheat the oven to 200°C (400°F) Gas 6.

Cut the tomatoes in half and lay in a sheet pan with sides with the garlic. Add the marinated lamb and 1 tablespoon of the marinade. Bake in the preheated oven for 15–20 minutes, uncovered, then stir in the beans, basil, olive oil, salt and pepper and crush the softened garlic cloves with the back of a fork as you stir, then taste to check the seasonings.

Put the sheet pan back into the oven with the heat turned off to allow the residual heat to heat the beans. Serve after 5 minutes.

PERFECT ROAST LAMB CHOPS WITH ROSEMARY VEGETABLES

A light but aromatic lamb dish to be enjoyed all year round. These chops are delicious.

8 lamb chops
1½ teaspoons sea salt
500 g/1 lb 2 oz. small new
    potatoes
2 sprigs of fresh rosemary,
    chopped in half
1 tablespoon olive oil

2 garlic cloves, peeled
400 g/14 oz. cherry tomatoes
250 g/9 oz. portabella
    mushrooms, thinly sliced
1 tablespoon balsamic glaze

SERVES 4

Preheat the oven to 220°C (425°F) Gas 7.

Put the lamb chops in a shallow bowl and sprinkle over 1 teaspoon of the salt. Set aside.

Place the potatoes and rosemary in a large sheet pan with sides. Sprinkle the remaining salt over the potatoes, then drizzle over the olive oil. Bake in the preheated oven for 20 minutes.

Add the lamb chops and garlic cloves to the pan and bake for a further 20 minutes. With 10 minutes baking time to go, add the tomatoes and mushrooms to the pan with the balsamic glaze and give everything a stir. Serve when cooked.

7-HOUR LAMB WITH ROASTED CARROTS & CELERIAC

This succulent lamb dish requires very little preparation, but it does take a while to cook. The wait, however, is truly worth it. The earthy sweetness of the slow roasted carrots and celeriac complement the lamb perfectly. If you're missing some greens, you could stir some spinach into the juices once reduced and allow it to wilt before serving.

1 tablespoon sea salt
1 whole leg of lamb (bone in), roughly 2 kg/4½ lb.
1 tablespoon olive oil
4 large carrots, sliced into 2–3-cm/¾–1¼-in. thick rounds
1 celeriac, peeled and diced
300 ml/1¼ cups dry white wine
300 ml/1¼ cups stock (meat or vegetable)

SERVES 8

Preheat the oven to 120°C (250°F) Gas ½.

Sprinkle the salt evenly over the lamb. Place a sheet pan with high sides on the hob and heat the olive oil. Add the lamb to the sheet pan and sear on all sides until it reaches a lovely brown colour all over. Pour off the excess fat. Add the vegetables to the sheet pan, ensuring everything fits snugly.

Pour the wine and stock into the sheet pan. Put the sheet pan back on the hob and bring to the boil over medium heat.

Using oven gloves, cover the sheet pan tightly with foil, then place into the preheated oven for 7 hours until cooked, basting twice during the cooking time.

Remove the lamb and vegetables from the sheet pan, place on a warmed plate and cover in foil. Heat the juices on the hob again to reduce.

Carve the lamb and serve with the cooked vegetables and a little of the reduced juices over the top.

HONEY MUSTARD LAMB & PARSNIPS

A delightful mix of honey and mustard that serves to keep this lamb moist and flavoursome. A quick-win as far as roasts go too. One to impress. Serve with Twice Baked Cheesy Potatoes (page 135) for a substantial winter warmer.

½ leg of lamb, roughly 1 kg/2¼ lb.
60 ml/¼ cup tamari
2 tablespoons honey
1½ tablespoons wholegrain mustard
2 tablespoons warm water
5 parsnips, peeled and sliced
    lengthways into thirds
4 sprigs of fresh rosemary

SERVES 4

Take the lamb out of the refrigerator an hour before you are ready to cook it.

To make the marinade, mix the tamari, honey, mustard and warm water together in a bowl.

Put the lamb on a sheet pan with high sides and pour the marinade over the top. Leave to marinate for 1 hour, turning over a couple of times whilst marinating.

Preheat the oven to 200°C (400°F) Gas 6.

Put the parsnips and rosemary in the sheet pan with the lamb and tuck under the lamb. Spoon a little of the marinade over the lamb.

Put the sheet pan in the preheated oven and roast the lamb for about 55 minutes for rare adding another 10 minutes for medium.

Remove the lamb from the oven and leave to rest, covered in foil, for 10 minutes, before serving with the parsnips. The parsnips can remain in the oven in the residual heat whilst the lamb rests.

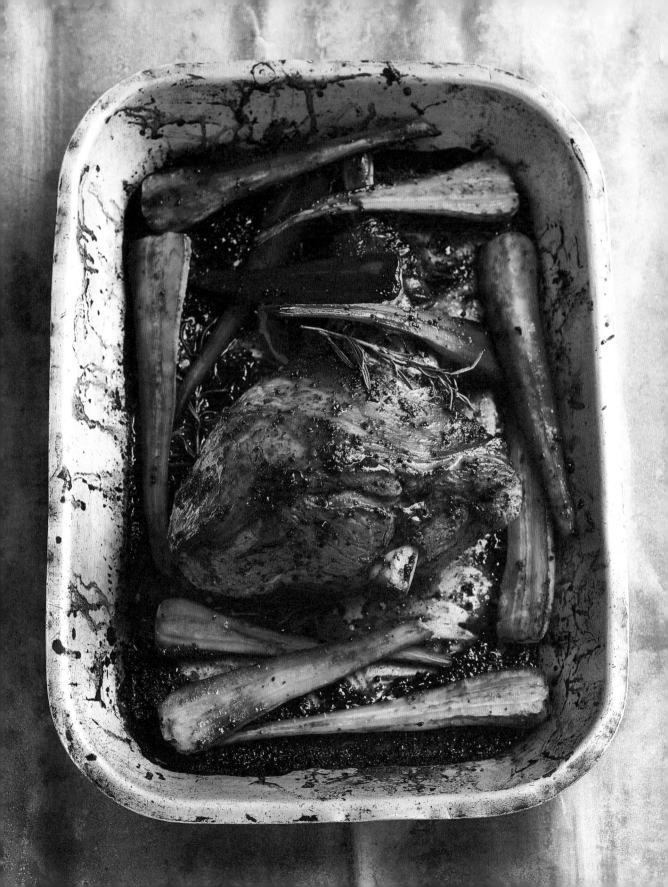

POULTRY

COQ AU VIN

This is a lighter version of the more wintry classic dish made with red wine. This dish is made using white wine, keeping it more summery. A family favourite!

250 g/9 oz. diced unsmoked
    streaky bacon
6 banana shallots, halved
3 garlic cloves, crushed
1 tablespoon freshly chopped
    thyme leaves
3 sprigs of fresh rosemary
8 chicken thighs (skin on), cut in two
    if large
3 tablespoons olive oil
250 ml/1 cup plus 1 tablespoon
    dry white wine
350 g/12 oz. mushrooms, cut
    into quarters
1 x 400-g/14-oz. can white beans, such
    as cannellini, drained and rinsed
sea salt
2 tablespoons freshly chopped flat leaf
    parsley, to serve

SERVES 4

Preheat the oven to 200°C (400°F) Gas 6.

Toss the bacon, shallots, garlic, thyme and rosemary into a sheet pan with sides. Arrange the chicken thighs on top.

Season with salt and drizzle over the olive oil.

Roast in the preheated oven for 20 minutes. Add the wine, mushrooms and white beans and give everything a stir, then roast for another 25 minutes until the chicken is cooked through. Serve, sprinkled with the parsley.

SPANISH RED PEPPER & CHICKEN BAKE

8–10 new potatoes, cut into quarters,
    lengthways
1 teaspoon olive oil
1 teaspoon sea salt
1 onion, finely chopped
1 garlic clove, finely chopped
1 red (bell) pepper, deseeded and
    very finely chopped
½ teaspoon marjoram or oregano
¾ teaspoon smoked paprika
1 x 400-g/14-oz. can chopped tomatoes
200 g/7 oz. mini chicken fillets
1 tablespoon freshly chopped oregano

SERVES 2

This is a dish that tastes of Spanish holidays. It cooks whilst you plan your next summer vacation.

Preheat the oven to 200°C (400°F) Gas 6.

Put the potatoes on a small sheet pan with sides, drizzle over the olive oil and sprinkle over ¼ teaspoon salt.

Bake in the preheated oven for 20 minutes. Make sure the potatoes are almost cooked. If not, give them a little longer.

Meanwhile, make the sauce. Combine the onion, garlic, red (bell) pepper, herbs, paprika, the remaining salt and tomatoes in a bowl. Add the chicken and the sauce to the potatoes, then cover with foil and cook in the oven for a further 20 minutes until the chicken is cooked. Sprinkle over the freshly chopped oregano, if desired, and serve.

HARISSA CHICKEN & CHICKPEA BAKE

Succulent spicy chicken and soft melt-in-the-mouth chickpeas, this is a protein-rich meal that feels rather more luxurious than the ingredients would tell us otherwise.

500 g/1 lb. 2 oz. skinless, boneless chicken
    breasts, cut into 4-cm/1½-in. pieces
1 courgette/zucchini, sliced into
    5 mm/¼-in. rounds
1 onion, cut into 16 slices
2 large, flat mushrooms, thickly sliced
1 teaspoon olive oil
½ teaspoon sea salt
1 x 400-g/14-oz. can chickpeas,
    drained and rinsed

for the marinade
1 tablespoon honey or maple syrup
1½ teaspoons harissa spice mix
2 tablespoons olive oil
½ teaspoon sea salt

SERVES 4

Preheat the oven to 220°C (425°F) Gas 7.

First make the marinade. Mix the marinade ingredients together in a large bowl. Put the chopped chicken in the bowl with the marinade and stir to coat. Set aside.

Place the courgette/zucchini, onion and mushrooms on a sheet pan with sides, drizzle over the olive oil and sprinkle over the salt. Bake in the preheated oven for 20 minutes, stirring once during baking.

Add the marinated chicken and the marinade to the sheet pan and give everything a good stir. Bake for about 15 minutes more until the chicken is cooked. Check the chicken to see if it is cooked. If not, leave it in the oven for a little longer.

Finally, stir in the chickpeas and place back in the oven for a couple of minutes to warm through. Serve immediately.

CORNFLAKE CHICKEN NUGGETS WITH SWEET POTATO CHIPS & ROASTED CHERRY TOMATOES

One of my children has a friend who really prefers classic children's foods to a range of adult flavours so when she comes round I tend to modify our recipes a little. These nuggets were, according to her, 'the best nuggets I have ever tasted'. I am taking that as a compliment!

2 medium sweet potatoes, peeled and sliced
    into 1-cm/½-in. thick chips/fries
1 teaspoon olive oil
¾ teaspoon sea salt
120 g/5 cups cornflakes
1 egg
125 ml/½ cup dairy or non-dairy milk
1 tablespoon arrowroot powder
¼ teaspoon garlic salt
4 skinless, boneless chicken breasts, chopped
    into 4 x 2-cm/1½ x ¾-in. nuggets
16 cherry tomatoes on the vine

SERVES 4

Preheat the oven to 200°C (400°F) Gas 6.

Put the sweet potatoes on a sheet pan with sides, drizzle over the olive oil and sprinkle over ½ teaspoon salt. Bake in the preheated oven for 35 minutes.

Meanwhile, grind the cornflakes in a food processor to fine crumbs. Alternatively, put the cornflakes in a freezer bag, close the bag tightly and bash the cornflakes with a rolling pin. Place in a bowl.

In another small bowl, whisk the egg, add the milk, arrowroot, garlic salt and ¼ teaspoon salt.

Dip the chicken nuggets into the egg mixture, then into the cornflakes to cover and put onto a separate sheet pan. Put the chicken nuggets in the oven with the potatoes for the last 10 minutes of baking. Add the tomatoes to the sweet potato sheet pan for the last 10 minutes. Serve immediately.

CHICKEN NUGGETS WITH ROASTED TOMATOES, OLIVES & ASPARAGUS

This is a fantastically simple gluten-free chicken nugget recipe that's quick to make and complemented by moist and succulent baked tomatoes, olives and asparagus.

600 g/3½ cups cherry tomatoes, halved
20 asparagus tips
6 garlic cloves, halved
1 tablespoon olive oil
½ teaspoon sea salt
2 x 85-g/3-oz. bags plantain chips
2 teaspoons garlic powder
1 x 190-g/7-oz. jar red pesto
4 skinless, boneless chicken breasts,
    sliced into mini fillets
1 x 190-g/7-oz. jar pitted black olives,
    drained (110-g/4-oz. drained weight)

SERVES 4

Preheat the oven to 200°C (400°F) Gas 6.

Spread the tomatoes and asparagus out on a sheet pan with sides and scatter over the garlic cloves. Drizzle over the olive oil and sprinkle over the salt. Roast in the preheated oven for 15 minutes.

To make the chicken nuggets, crush the plantain chips into a breadcrumb consistency in a food processor or in a plastic bag with a rolling pin. Put the plantain crumbs into a bowl and stir in the garlic powder. Put the red pesto in a separate bowl. Dip each mini chicken fillet into the red pesto, then into the crushed plantain/garlic powder mix to coat.

When the tomatoes and asparagus have been baking for 15 minutes, add the olives to the pan, and place the chicken nuggets on a separate sheet pan and bake for a further 12 minutes. Check the nuggets are cooked through. Serve.

CHEAT'S CHICKEN KIEV WITH TOMATOES, COURGETTES & ROASTED NEW POTATOES

Kids will love this! It's a lot like the processed version in taste except this version is real. Believe me when I say that they'll not miss the breadcrumbs.

20 medium new potatoes, diced into 15-mm/⅝-in. cubes
1 tablespoon olive oil
4 skinless, boneless chicken breasts
2 garlic cloves, peeled
10 g/½ cup fresh flat leaf parsley, including stalks
60 g/4 tablespoons salted butter, softened
12 cherry tomatoes
1 courgette/zucchini, cut into 1-cm/½-in. thick slices
½ teaspoon garlic salt

SERVES 4

Preheat the oven to 200°C (400°F) Gas 6.

Place the new potatoes on a sheet pan, add the olive oil and mix to coat.

Create four foil or baking parchment rectangles (with enough excess to fold over the chicken) and place a chicken breast on each. Using a sharp knife, slice down the length of the top of the chicken breasts, but don't cut right through them.

In a food processor, finely chop the garlic and parsley and then mix in the butter. Divide the mixture between the chicken breast pockets.

Add three cherry tomatoes and some courgette/zucchini slices to each parcel and sprinkle over the garlic salt. Close the parcels up, then nestle them in amongst the potatoes, clearing potatoes out from under each parcel on the sheet pan. Bake in the preheated oven for 30–35 minutes until the potatoes and chicken breasts are cooked through.

Serving Suggestion: Serve with baked sweet potatoes.

ROASTED CHICKEN THIGHS WITH PLUMS & TARRAGON

There's an invasion of Scandinavian influence in the UK right now and I, for one, welcome it, especially when it means cheap quality furniture and some unusual but delicious culinary influences too. This combination of chicken, plums and tarragon is inspired by a Scandinavian original.

8 chicken thighs
2 teaspoons garlic salt
20 g/1 cup fresh tarragon
4 large plums, halved and stoned/pitted
5 shallots, halved
1 head of broccoli, cut into florets
2 teaspoons olive oil
freshly ground black pepper

SERVES 4

Preheat the oven to 190°C (375°F) Gas 5.

Put the chicken pieces on a sheet pan with deep sides. Add the garlic salt, tarragon, plums, shallots and pepper, to taste.

Bake in the preheated oven for 45–50 minutes until the chicken is cooked through.

With 20 minutes to go, add the broccoli to the pan, drizzle over the olive oil and continue to bake. Serve.

CHICKEN FAJITAS WITH MILD GUACAMOLE

This is a very popular and sociable meal. Simply lay all of the elements out on the table and let people help themselves. Try stopping my two children from going back for seconds and thirds of this dish!

800 g/1¾ lb. boneless, skinless chicken breasts, cut into strips
2 orange (bell) peppers, deseeded and sliced
2 courgettes/zucchini, sliced
2 onions, halved and sliced
1 x 28-g/1-oz. pack fajita seasoning (try and avoid the ones that have sugar as their prime ingredient)
4 tablespoons olive oil
8 tortilla wraps or lettuce leaves

for the guacamole
2 ripe avocados, peeled and stoned/pitted
5 g/¼ cup fresh coriander/cilantro, stems and leaves
70 g/2½ oz. red onion, finely diced
½ tablespoon freshly squeezed lime juice
1 plum tomato, peeled and deseeded
40 g/4 tablespoons extra virgin olive oil
sea salt and freshly ground black pepper, to taste
lime wedges, to serve

SERVES 4

Preheat the oven to 220°C (425°F) Gas 7.

In a large bowl, mix together the chicken strips, (bell) peppers, courgettes/zucchini and onions. In a separate bowl, mix the fajita seasoning and olive oil, then combine the seasoning/oil mix with the chicken mix and stir to make sure everything is coated evenly.

Spread this mix out on a large sheet pan.

Bake in the preheated oven for 15 minutes or until the chicken is cooked through and the vegetables are soft, stirring once.

Meanwhile, make the guacamole. Put all the guacamole ingredients into a food processor and blend.

Finally, just before you remove the chicken and vegetables from the oven, warm the tortillas or prepare the lettuce leaves. Serve the fajita chicken and vegetables with the guacamole and the wraps/lettuce leaves. Serve with lime wedges for squeezing over.

MOROCCAN CHICKEN

The root vegetables and apples in this recipe serve not only to soak up the delicious cooking juices from the chicken but also to provide a contrast in texture and flavour to the gentle Moroccan spices.

1 large oven-ready chicken
  (approx. 1.7 kg/3¾ lb.)
2½ teaspoons sea salt
500 g/1 lb. 2 oz. carrots,
  quartered lengthways
500 g/1 lb. 2 oz. sweet potatoes,
  peeled and cut into 15 mm/
  ⅝-in. discs
3 Granny Smith apples, quartered
  and cored

zest and juice of 1 large orange
250 ml/generous 1 cup
  chicken stock
250 ml/generous 1 cup dry
  white wine
1 tablespoon grated (peeled)
  fresh ginger
2 teaspoons ras-el-hanout
  or a Moroccan spice mix

SERVES 4

Preheat the oven to 200°C (400°F) Gas 6.

Find a roasting pan large enough for the chicken, vegetables, fruit and liquid to fit in. Put the chicken in the roasting pan. Season the skin of the chicken with the salt. Arrange the carrots, sweet potatoes and apples around the chicken.

Mix the orange zest and juice, stock, wine, ginger and ras-el-hanout together in a bowl and pour over the chicken and vegetables.

Bake in the preheated oven for 1 hour 25 minutes, basting frequently. Cover the chicken with foil after half the cooking time to ensure the outside is not overcooked. Serve whilst hot.

ROAST CHICKEN & BEANS WITH ROOT VEGETABLES

This dish is what my husband describes as 'a proper feed'. It's a tasty, filling all-in-one dish, combining winter vegetables and white beans with succulent roasted chicken. A dish that can be made for any occasion.

3 tablespoons olive oil
1 large oven-ready chicken (approx.
  1.7 kg/3¾ lb.)
1 lemon, halved
2 large leeks, thickly sliced
½ swede/rutabaga, peeled and diced
  into 1-cm/½-in. cubes
6 baby parsnips or 2 large parsnips,
  peeled and sliced into 6 x 2 cm/
  2½ x ¾-in. fingers
500 g/1 lb. 2 oz. Brussels sprouts
  (untrimmed weight), trimmed and halved
4 large garlic cloves, halved
1 tablespoon plus 1 teaspoon balsamic glaze
2 tablespoons freshly chopped thyme leaves
1 x 400-g/14-oz. can white beans,
  drained and rinsed
sea salt and freshly ground black pepper

SERVES 6

Preheat the oven to 200°C (400°F) Gas 6.

Heat 1 tablespoon of the olive oil in a very large sheet pan with sides (a large joint roasting pan should work here) in the preheated oven for 3 minutes. Add the whole chicken, placing it skin-side down initially, then immediately turn it over and rest breast-side up on the sheet pan. Season generously with salt and pepper and place the lemon halves inside the cavity of the chicken.

Put the chicken in the preheated oven and roast for 1 hour 25 minutes.

Put all of the prepared vegetables and garlic into a large bowl and stir in another 1 tablespoon of the olive oil and 1 tablespoon of the balsamic glaze with a pinch of salt, a twist of pepper and the chopped thyme.

50 minutes before the end of the chicken's roasting time, add the vegetables to the sheet pan and baste the chicken with the juices. Stir twice and baste the chicken twice more whilst they both cook. Take the chicken out of the sheet pan, stir in the beans and the remaining balsamic glaze and let them sit in the oven with the door shut and the oven turned off to heat through. Carve the chicken, then remove the vegetable/beans from the oven and serve.

GARLIC ROASTED CHICKEN WITH SHALLOTS & CARROTS

Soft and succulent roasted chicken and sweet roasted shallots and carrots is a winning combination for a celebration meal.

500 g/1 lb. 2 oz. carrots, sliced in half
400 g/14 oz. shallots, halved lengthways
1 large garlic bulb, sliced in half horizontally
1.5 kg/3¼ lb. whole chicken
70 g/5 tablespoons butter or ghee
  (at room temperature)
1½ tablespoons dry white wine
200 ml/generous ¾ cup fresh chicken stock
150 g/5½ oz. baby spinach
sea salt and freshly ground black pepper

SERVES 4-6

Preheat the oven to 200°C (400°F) Gas 6.

Put the carrots, shallots, garlic and chicken into a roasting pan. Smother the chicken with the butter or ghee and season well with salt and pepper.

Roast in the preheated oven for 45 minutes, basting twice.

Meanwhile, place the wine and stock in a large saucepan and stir. After 45 minutes, add the vegetables from the chicken pan to this pan and remove the garlic. Squeeze the soft garlic pulp out into the vegetable/stock mixture and discard the skin.

Cover the chicken with foil and roast for a further 30 minutes, basting once.

Heat the saucepan with the wine, stock and vegetables in and simmer gently for the remainder of the chicken roasting time. Add the spinach and stir until wilted. Remove from the heat.

Check that the chicken is cooked through, then leave it to rest. Carve and serve the chicken with some of the cooked veg and a little of the stock over the top.

Serving Suggestion: Serve with Perfect Roasted Potatoes (page 135).

DUCK IN ORANGE GLAZE ON A BED OF LEEKS & MUSHROOMS

This dish is a modern take on the heavy and sugary duck à l'orange of the 1980s. The duck combines with melt-in-the-mouth leeks and mushrooms. A fine dish!

freshly squeezed juice of ½ orange
3 heaped tablespoons St. Dalfour Thick Cut Orange Spread/bitter Seville orange marmalade
1 teaspoon red wine vinegar
2 boneless duck breasts, each about 170 g/6 oz., skin on
2 large leeks, cut in half lengthways and into 1-cm/½-in. slices
200 g/7 oz. chestnut mushrooms, halved
sea salt and freshly ground black pepper

SERVES 2

Preheat the oven to 190°C (375°F) Gas 5.

In a small bowl, mix together the orange juice, orange spread and vinegar, plus some salt and pepper, to create a glaze.

Lay the duck breasts skin-side up in a sheet pan and spread the glaze over the top. Leave to marinate whilst you prepare your vegetables.

Put the vegetables in the sheet pan alongside the duck and give the vegetables a good stir. Season with salt and pepper.

Bake in the preheated oven for 30 minutes, but baste the duck breasts once and stir the vegetables well to make sure they are cooking evenly. Serve.

DUCK LEGS WITH APPLE, PARSNIP & WHITE CABBAGE

This is a substantial winter dish. When you need comfort, look straight over at this recipe. Sweet and succulent duck combines with moist and flavoursome cabbage that has been allowed to soak up an abundance of flavour from the rest of the dish.

4 duck legs
1 tablespoon sea salt
5 large parsnips, peeled and halved
1 white cabbage, cored and cut into 10 portions
4 Granny Smith apples, halved and cored
½ teaspoon ground cloves
½ teaspoon ground allspice

SERVES 4

Preheat the oven to 180°C (350°F) Gas 4.

Place the duck legs in a large roasting pan and season well with the salt.

Bake in the preheated oven for 20 minutes, then baste with the juices released from the legs and add the vegetables and apples, turning those over in the juices too. Sprinkle the spices over the dish.

Bake for another 1 hour 20 minutes, turning the vegetables and legs three times whilst cooking. Serve.

Serving Suggestion: Serve with a green salad.

THAI SALMON BAKE

Whilst salmon is one of our prime sources of omega-3 fatty acids, it is not always everyone's favourite. Baking it in this light Thai sauce adds flavour but also helps to keep the salmon really moist. It should simply fall apart when a fork is pushed into it. You can make this spicier if palates in your household prefer.

2 garlic cloves, crushed

2-cm/¾-in. piece of ginger, peeled and finely chopped

1 x 400-g/14-oz. can coconut milk

1 tablespoon unrefined or coconut sugar

1½ teaspoons Thai 7 Spice seasoning

2 tablespoons fish sauce

1 tablespoon freshly squeezed lime juice

3 banana shallots, finely chopped

2 tablespoons freshly chopped coriander/cilantro

4 salmon fillets (approx. 140 g/5 oz.), skin on

250 g/9 oz. asparagus spears, cut into 2-cm/¾-in. pieces

SERVES 4

Preheat the oven to 200°C (400°F) Gas 6.

Put the garlic, ginger, coconut milk, sugar, Thai 7 Spice seasoning, fish sauce and lime juice in a medium-sized bowl and mix together. Add the shallots and coriander/cilantro to the mixture. Alternatively, put the garlic, ginger, shallots and coriander into a food processor and chop, then add the coconut milk, fish sauce, sugar, Thai 7 Spice seasoning and lime juice and mix again.

Put the salmon, skin side down, and the asparagus slices on a sheet pan.

Pour the sauce mix over the top of the salmon and asparagus. Cover with foil and bake in the preheated oven for 35 minutes. Serve.

Note if using wild salmon, you may want to add this 15 minutes into the cooking time to keep it moist, as wild salmon naturally contains less fat.

Serving Suggestion: Serve with boiled basmati rice or quinoa.

SMOKED SALMON MUFFINS

If you are a fan of salmon and scrambled eggs, then you'll love these muffins. They're light and delicious. A mix of salmon saltiness and smooth creamy egg with a snap of chive. They're great hot or cold.

4 eggs

100 g/3½ oz. smoked salmon, roughly chopped

2 spring onions/scallions, sliced into 5-mm/¼-in. pieces

1 tablespoon grated Parmesan or Pecorino cheese

¼ teaspoon freshly ground black pepper

muffin pan, lightly greased with olive oil

SERVES 2

Preheat the oven to 200°C (400°F) Gas 6.

Put the eggs, salmon, spring onions/scallions, cheese and black pepper in a bowl and whisk together.

Pour an equal amount of the mixture into four of the muffin pan holes.

Bake in the preheated oven for 15–20 minutes until the muffins are fully cooked with no runny egg present. Serve.

Serving Suggestion: Serve with slices of avocado and fresh tomatoes, with a little chopped fresh basil, olive oil, salt and pepper over the top.

TOMATO PESTO HALIBUT WITH GREEN VEG

Packed full of flavour, this tomato pesto topping really brings the halibut to life.
It's quick to create the pesto and simple to make the dish.

250 g/9 oz. asparagus tips
300 g/10½ oz. tenderstem
    broccoli
1 large courgette/zucchini,
    cut into 2-cm/¾-in. pieces
1 tablespoon olive oil
4 halibut fillets, skin on, approx.
    2.5-cm/1-in. thick (each about
    200 g/7 oz.)
sea salt and freshly ground
    black pepper

for the tomato pesto
60 g/4 cups fresh basil leaves
70 g/½ cup walnuts, toasted
110 g/1 cup sun-dried tomatoes
    in oil, drained
1 large garlic clove, peeled
5 tablespoons olive oil

SERVES 4

Preheat the oven to 200°C (400°F) Gas 6.

For the pesto, combine the basil leaves, toasted walnuts, sun-dried tomatoes and garlic in a food processor then add the olive oil and combine again to make a paste.

Put the vegetables on a sheet pan, drizzle over the olive oil and season with salt and pepper. Bake in the preheated oven for 20 minutes.

Meanwhile, create four foil or baking parchment parcels. Put one halibut fillet into each parcel and cover each fillet with a thick layer of the tomato pesto. Close up the parcels and put them on the sheet pan with the vegetables. Bake both the vegetables and fish for a further 12 minutes.

Check the fish is just cooked, then serve immediately.

MEDITERRANEAN BAKED FISH FILLETS

This is a simple summer all-in-one fish dish that you'll enjoy eating in the sun
(if you can find some).

8 cherry tomatoes, thinly sliced
6 spring onions/scallions, thinly
    sliced on the diagonal
1 tablespoon freshly chopped
    parsley
1 courgette/zucchini, very
    thinly sliced
freshly squeezed juice
    of ½ lemon

2 tablespoons fish stock
    or dry white wine
1 tablespoon olive oil
1½ teaspoons sea salt
3 white fish fillets

SERVES 3

Preheat the oven to 200°C (400°F) Gas 6.

Put the sliced tomatoes, spring onions/scallions, parsley, courgette/zucchini, lemon juice, stock or white wine, olive oil and salt in a bowl and mix together.

Create three foil or baking parchment parcels. Put one fish fillet in each parcel and top with the tomato mix.

Close up the parcels tightly, put them on a sheet pan and bake in the preheated oven for 20 minutes until cooked.

Remove from the oven and serve with a green salad.

COD BAKED IN TOMATO & OLIVE SAUCE

The sauce in this fish recipe keeps the dish deliciously moist and seeps into the cod fillets, making them even more succulent. A great dish for reluctant fish eaters!

2 onions, finely chopped
2 garlic cloves, finely chopped
10 g/6 tablespoons freshly chopped parsley
600 g/1 lb. 5 oz. canned chopped tomatoes
1 teaspoon sea salt
4 medium cod fillets
2 courgettes/zucchini, very thinly sliced
100 g/1 cup pitted green olives
2 teaspoons olive oil

SERVES 4

Preheat the oven to 200°C (400°F) Gas 6.

Put the onion, garlic and parsley in a medium-sized bowl, mix together, then add the chopped tomatoes and salt and stir to combine.

Put the cod fillets on a sheet pan with deep sides. Pour some of the tomato mixture over the top. Add the courgettes/zucchini and olives to the sheet pan and cover in the remaining tomato mixture. Drizzle over the olive oil.

Bake in the preheated oven for 10–15 minutes until the cod fillets are just cooked. Serve.

Serving Suggestion: Serve with a green salad.

COD LOIN WITH BALSAMIC FENNEL

Whilst fennel is a love it or hate it kind of vegetable, with the addition of balsamic glaze and alongside baked cod, this dish really comes alive. You may even discover that not as many people dislike fennel as claim they do.

2 fennel bulbs, sliced into
    2-cm/¾-in. wedges
1 tablespoon balsamic glaze
2 tablespoons olive oil
2 teaspoons sea salt
4 thick cod loins
1 x 400-g/14-oz. can cherry tomatoes
1 teaspoon coconut sugar or honey
3 tablespoons freshly chopped parsley
freshly ground black pepper

SERVES 4

Preheat the oven to 220°C (425°F) Gas 7.

Put the fennel wedges on a sheet pan. Drizzle over the balsamic glaze, 1 tablespoon of the olive oil and 1 teaspoon salt. Bake in the preheated oven for 15 minutes. Toss once during baking.

Meanwhile, lay the fish on a smaller sheet pan with sides so that the fillets fit snugly.

Pour over the cherry tomatoes, coconut sugar or honey, chopped parsley, the remaining 1 tablespoon olive oil and 1 teaspoon salt and a pinch of pepper.

Bake for a further 15–20 minutes until the fish is cooked through and the fennel is crisp at the edges. Serve.

LEMON & BUTTER BAKED SALMON WITH SPRING VEGETABLES

'Spring' and 'simple' are the words that come to mind with this meal. It's all about simple flavours and even simpler techniques, and it celebrates the flavours of Spring!

8 new potatoes, cut into 1-cm/½-in. pieces
1½ teaspoons olive oil
1 teaspoon sea salt
8 asparagus spears, trimmed
10 cherry tomatoes
6 mushrooms, chopped into quarters
2 salmon fillets
40 g/3 tablespoons butter
2 lemon slices
freshly ground black pepper

SERVES 2

Preheat the oven to 200°C (400°F) Gas 6.

Lay the potatoes on a sheet pan. Drizzle over the olive oil and sprinkle over ½ teaspoon of the salt. Bake in the preheated oven for 10 minutes.

Add the asparagus, tomatoes and mushrooms to the sheet pan and stir. Bake for a further 10 minutes.

Add the salmon fillets with a large knob of butter and a slice of lemon on top of each, and sprinkle over the remaining salt and some black pepper.

Bake for a further 10–12 minutes until the salmon is just cooked. Serve.

WHITE FISH & CHORIZO BAKE

This is an ideal surf and turf meal. Spicy chorizo combined with mellow white fish gives this dish a real depth of flavour.

1 red (bell) pepper, deseeded and
    thinly sliced
1 red onion, thinly sliced
1 courgette/zucchini, cut into
    1-cm/½-in. slices
1½ teaspoons olive oil
75 g/½ cup finely chopped chorizo
1 lemon, quartered lengthways
2 vines of cherry tomatoes (about
    10 on each)
2 white fish fillets
1 teaspoon smoked paprika
¾ teaspoon sea salt
freshly chopped parsley, to garnish

SERVES 2

Preheat the oven to 200°C (400°F) Gas 6.

Put the (bell) pepper, onion and courgette/zucchini on a sheet pan and drizzle over the olive oil. Stir the vegetables, then bake in the preheated oven for 20 minutes.

Remove the sheet pan from the oven and add the chorizo and lemon quarters, then the vine tomatoes and fish fillets on top. Sprinkle over the paprika and salt and bake for a further 12 minutes. Remove from the oven and check the fish is just cooked, then serve. If the fish is not cooked, then leave in the oven for up to 4 more minutes to cook through. Sprinkle over the parsley, to garnish.

CAJUN SALMON WITH CRISPY LEEKS & BUTTERNUT SQUASH

Wham, bam, thank you mam! This dish is a flavour-packed way to enjoy omega-3 rich salmon. Only ever so slightly spicy and the Cajun spices contrast well with the mellow leeks and baked squash.

2 leeks, sliced lengthways, then into 15-mm/⅝-in. thick semi-circles
½ butternut squash, peeled, deseeded and cut into 1-cm/½-in. cubes
1 tablespoon plus 2 teaspoons olive oil
1¾ teaspoons sea salt
1 teaspoon smoked paprika
1 teaspoon coconut or unrefined sugar
1 garlic clove, crushed
½ teaspoon onion powder
½ teaspoon mustard powder
½ teaspoon finely grated lemon zest
⅛ teaspoon dried marjoram or oregano
⅛ teaspoon dried thyme
1 teaspoon red wine vinegar
4 salmon fillets (about 125 g/4½ oz. each)
lemon wedges, to serve

SERVES 4

Preheat the oven to 200°C (400°F) Gas 6.

Put the vegetables on a sheet pan with sides with 1 tablespoon olive oil and 1 teaspoon salt and toss to mix.

Bake in the preheated oven for 20 minutes.

Meanwhile, prepare the topping for the salmon. In a bowl, mix together the smoked paprika, ¾ teaspoon salt, sugar, garlic, onion powder, mustard powder, lemon zest, herbs, red wine vinegar and 2 teaspoons olive oil.

Lay the salmon fillets out on a plate and smother each with an equal amount of the topping.

Add the salmon fillets to the sheet pan with the vegetables, and reduce the oven to 180°C (350°F) Gas 4. Bake for a further 15 minutes until cooked.

Serve the salmon on a bed of leeks and butternut squash with lemon wedges for squeezing.

INDIAN PRAWNS WITH CAULIFLOWER

Indian food is synonymous with both prawns/shrimp and cauliflower. Here the two are combined in a curry. It's mild and one to be lapped up by all family members.

1 cauliflower, chopped
  into florets
2 teaspoons sea salt
1 tablespoon olive oil
1 onion, finely chopped
1½ tablespoons freshly chopped
  coriander/cilantro
2 garlic cloves, crushed
5 mm/¼ in. finger of fresh
  ginger, peeled and grated
1 teaspoon ground cumin
½ teaspoon ground turmeric

¼ teaspoon ground coriander
⅛ teaspoon ground cinnamon
1 x 400-g/14-oz. can coconut
  milk
1 x 400-g/14-oz. can chopped
  tomatoes
225 g/8 oz. frozen king prawns/
  shrimp
1 tablespoon freshly chopped
  coriander/cilantro (optional)

SERVES 4

Preheat the oven to 200°C (400°F) Gas 6.

Place the cauliflower florets on a sheet pan with sides. Sprinkle over 1 teaspoon of the salt and drizzle over the olive oil. Bake in the preheated oven for 30 minutes.

Meanwhile, make the sauce with the onion, coriander/cilantro, garlic, ginger, spices, coconut milk, chopped tomatoes and the remaining salt. You can do this by mixing these ingredients in a bowl or preferably in a food processor.

Add the sauce and prawns/shrimp to the sheet pan, stir and bake for a further 20 minutes until cooked. Sprinkle over the freshly chopped coriander/cilantro, if using, and serve.

TAMARI & GINGER SALMON WITH ROASTED NEW POTATOES & ASPARAGUS

There's a little marinating time involved in this recipe if you can spare it. The best results will come from marinating all day. A little preparation in the morning will mean a greater tasting dish that evening. It's worth it too because the salmon will just flake away and each mouthful will provide the winning taste combination of honey, ginger and tamari.

4 salmon fillets
400 g/14 oz. baby new potatoes,
  cut to the same size as the
  smallest whole potato
1 teaspoon olive oil
⅛ teaspoon sea salt
150 g/5½ oz. fine asparagus tips,
  sliced into 2-cm/¾-in. lengths

for the marinade
70 ml/scant ⅓ cup tamari
1 generous tablespoon honey
2 garlic cloves, crushed
10 g/1 tablespoon freshly grated
  ginger (peeled)

SERVES 4

To make the marinade, combine the tamari, honey, garlic and ginger in a flat bowl. Add the salmon fillets to the bowl, turn to coat and ensure they are all sitting in the marinade. Cover the bowl and place in the refrigerator for 8 hours.

When you are ready to cook, preheat the oven to 200°C (400°F) Gas 6.

Prepare the potatoes and put them on a sheet pan with sides. Drizzle over the olive oil and sprinkle over the salt. Bake in the preheated oven for 20 minutes. Check they are almost soft on the inside, then add the salmon, 2 tablespoons of the marinade and the asparagus to the sheet pan.

Bake for a further 10–15 minutes until the salmon just flakes away when you push it down with a fork. Serve.

ROASTED MONKFISH & PARMA HAM PARCELS ON DILL POTATOES

Monkfish is a really substantial, almost 'meaty' fish, so even some non-fish-lovers will be converted by this dish. What better way to serve it than wrapped in salty Parma ham/prosciutto with summery dill potatoes and courgettes/zucchini?

500 g/1 lb. 2 oz. new potatoes, washed and quartered
1 tablespoon olive oil
1 teaspoon sea salt
1 medium courgette/zucchini, sliced lengthways and into 1.5-cm/½-in. thick semi-circles
1 teaspoon dried dill or 2 teaspoons freshly chopped dill
4 skinless, boneless monkfish portions, approx. 140–150 g/5–5½ oz. each
8 sun-dried tomato slices, from a jar in oil, drained and thinly sliced
2 teaspoons butter
1 tablespoon freshly squeezed lemon juice
¼ teaspoon cracked black pepper
8 slices of Parma ham/prosciutto

SERVES 4

Preheat the oven to 200°C (400°F) Gas 6.

Place the potatoes on a sheet pan with sides. Drizzle over ½ tablespoon of the olive oil and ½ teaspoon salt. Bake in the preheated oven for 15 minutes.

Add the courgette/zucchini to the pan containing the potatoes. Add the remaining olive oil and salt and the dill and stir. Bake the potatoes and courgettes/zucchini for another 10 minutes.

Meanwhile, prepare the fish. Create a deep incision along the top of each fish portion and tuck some of the sun-dried tomato slices and ½ teaspoon of butter. Squeeze over the lemon juice, sprinkle over the black pepper, then wrap each portion in two slices of Parma ham/prosciutto.

Place the fish parcels onto the sheet pan and bake for another 10 minutes or until the fish is just cooked.

Serve immediately.

VEGETARIAN

BLACK BEAN & SWEETCORN HASH

This hash is all about texture. With each mouthful your mouth explodes with the sweet kernels of corn that contrast with the smooth, soft and satisfying black beans. A rainbow of colours is on show with this dish. It's a nice one to serve in the middle of the table and let people help themselves.

2 medium sweet potatoes, peeled
   and cut into 1.5-cm/½-in. cubes
1 medium courgette/zucchini, cut
   into 1.5-cm/½-in. cubes
1 red (bell) pepper, cut into
   1.5-cm/⅝-in. pieces
4 large mushrooms, cut into
   1.5-cm/½-in. cubes
1 x 400-g/14-oz. can black beans,
   drained and rinsed
130 g/15 oz. canned sweetcorn
3 tablespoons olive oil
¾ teaspoon garlic salt
½ teaspoon sea salt
1 teaspoon sweet smoked paprika
4 eggs
freshly ground black pepper

SERVES 2
AS A MAIN MEAL

Preheat the oven to 200°C (400°F) Gas 6.

Place the sweet potatoes, courgette/ zucchini, (bell) pepper, mushrooms, black beans and sweetcorn onto a sheet pan with sides.

Drizzle over the olive oil, sprinkle over the garlic salt, salt and paprika and give everything a good stir. Bake in the preheated oven for 30 minutes. Stir once during cooking.

Remove from the oven after 30 minutes, make four wells in the vegetables then crack an egg into each well.

Bake for a further 7–9 minutes until the eggs are just cooked but the yolks are still runny. Season with black pepper and serve.

PURPLE SPROUTING BROCCOLI & FLAGEOLET BEANS WITH PRESERVED LEMON MAYO

This easy-peasy combo of crispy, lightly charred broccoli, soft garlicky beans, crunchy lemony crumbs and zippy, unctuous preserved lemon mayo makes a fabulous light lunch.

350 g/12 oz. purple sprouting broccoli
1 x 400-g/14-oz. can flageolet beans
3 tablespoons olive oil
2 garlic cloves, finely chopped
a large handful of fresh parsley,
    finely chopped
3 tablespoons panko crumbs
zest of 1 lemon

for the mayo
1 egg
1 garlic clove, grated
1 tablespoon Dijon mustard
juice of ½ lemon
250 ml/1 cup plus 1 tablespoon sunflower oil
¼–½ preserved lemon

SERVES 4

To make the preserved lemon mayonnaise, put the egg, grated garlic, Dijon mustard and lemon juice into a jug/pitcher. Whiz everything together using a stick blender. Slowly add the oil, keeping the blender going and pouring in a steady stream, until all oil is incorporated and the mixture is thick and light.

Rinse the salt from the preserved lemon, remove the inner flesh and discard. Finely chop the softened skin and add it to the mayonnaise. Cover and refrigerate until ready to use.

Preheat the oven to 180°C (350°F) Gas 4. Trim the broccoli. Leave the stalks quite long, but peel away any tough bits using a vegetable peeler. Lay the broccoli over a sheet pan and cook for 10–15 minutes, until the broccoli is al dente, but starting to crisp on the florets. Drain and rinse the beans. Pop them into a bowl and add the oil, chopped garlic and parsley. Remove the broccoli from the oven and spoon the beans over. Mix the panko crumbs and lemon zest together and scatter this over the top. Return the sheet pan to the oven and cook for a further 5 minutes, until the beans are warmed through. Take care not to leave the pan in for too long, or the beans will dry and crack – they just need to be warm rather than super-hot. Serve with the preserved lemon mayo.

ROASTED RED CABBAGE WITH CHARRED BROCCOLI, CHERRIES & ALMONDS

1 red cabbage
4 tablespoons olive oil
600 g/21 oz. broccoli
50 g/½ cup toasted, flaked/slivered almonds
100 g/¾ cup dried cherries
a bunch of spring onions/scallions, chopped
a large bunch of fresh dill, coarsely chopped
sea salt and freshly ground black pepper

for the balsamic dressing
40 ml/3 tablespoons extra virgin olive oil
30 ml/2 tablespoons balsamic vinegar
1 teaspoon caster/granulated sugar
sea salt flakes
Oven-Roasted Chilli Jam (page 156), to serve

SERVES 4

Red cabbage and broccoli roast beautifully and have an awesome affinity with sweet, tangy balsamic vinegar dressing. Almonds and plump juicy dried cherries add flavour and crunch. I like this with Oven-Roasted Chilli Jam (page 156).

Preheat the oven to 200°C (400°F) Gas 6. Cut the red cabbage into wedges and arrange them over a sheet pan. Drizzle with the oil, season and roast for 10 minutes. Chop the broccoli very finely – to an almost rice-like texture – and scatter it around the wedges of cabbage. Sprinkle with flaked/slivered almonds, return the pan to the oven, and cook for a further 10 minutes.

Mix all the ingredients for the dressing together and season with salt flakes. Remove the pan from the oven and gently push the cooked almonds into the broccoli using a fork. Drizzle everything with the dressing and scatter with the dried cherries, chopped spring onions/scallions and dill. Serve with Oven-Roasted Chilli Jam (page 156).

CHERRY TOMATO, ROASTED PEPPER & SPINACH BOMBAY EGGS

When it comes to choosing my favourite cooked brunch dish, this lovely tomato-rich bake comes tops. It's a winner for a satisfying lunch or supper too.

for the chilli/chile oil
100 ml/⅓ cup plus 1 tablespoon extra virgin olive oil
1 tablespoon dried chilli/red pepper flakes

for the Bombay eggs
2 red onions, cut into wedges
1 red (bell) pepper, deseeded and cut into strips
1 yellow and 1 orange (bell) pepper, deseeded and cut into strips
3 tablespoons olive oil
2 teaspoons ground coriander
2 teaspoons ground cumin
1 teaspoon ground turmeric
500 g/18 oz. cherry tomatoes
600 ml/2½ cups passata/strained tomatoes
50 g/1¾ oz. fresh ginger root, peeled and finely grated
1 tablespoon caster/granulated sugar
1 teaspoon chilli/red pepper flakes
2–3 big handfuls of fresh baby spinach leaves
large bunch of fresh coriander/cilantro, coarsely chopped
4 eggs
150 ml/⅔ cup Greek or full-fat natural/plain yogurt
2 teaspoon nigella seeds (optional)
sea salt and freshly ground black pepper

SERVES 4

Combine the oil and chilli/red pepper flakes together in a screw-top jar. Set aside. Preheat the oven to 180°C (350°F) Gas 4. Scatter the onions and (bell) peppers over the base of a large roasting pan and drizzle with the oil. Cook for 20 minutes, until the vegetables begin to soften. Stir in the ground coriander, cumin and turmeric. Return the pan to the oven and cook for a further 10 minutes.

In the meantime, place the cherry tomatoes into a large bowl and pour in the passata. Stir in the grated ginger, sugar and chilli/red pepper flakes. Season with salt and freshly ground black pepper.

Remove the roasting pan from the oven and stir the tomato mix into the (bell) peppers. Return everything to the oven and bake for a further 30 minutes. Stir in the spinach leaves and half of the coriander/cilantro. Make four shallow indentations in the mixture and crack an egg into each. Return to the oven and cook for a further 5–7 minutes, until the eggs are just set. Remove from the oven and drizzle the yogurt over. Scatter over the leftover coriander/cilantro, add a sprinkling of nigella seeds, and drizzle with the chilli/chile oil. Serve with bread.

LEEK, RED PEPPER & BRIE STRATA

This is lovely with all sorts of different cheeses in place of the brie – punchier washed rind cheeses such as taleggio or zippy goats' cheeses work well, even a strong Cheddar – and feta is fabulous too.

2 large leeks, trimmed and sliced
3 red (bell) peppers, deseeded and cut into strips
3 tablespoons olive oil
300 g/10½ oz. (day old, if possible) crusty baguette
30 g/2 tablespoons butter
600 ml/2½ cups full-fat milk
6 eggs
2 tablespoons grain mustard
large handful of freshly chopped mixed herbs (tarragon, chives, parsley and dill are fab)
200 g/7 oz. brie, cut into bite-sized cubes

SERVES 4

Preheat the oven to 190°C (375°F) Gas 5. Scatter the leeks and (bell) peppers over the base of a large, deep, lightly greased sheet pan. Drizzle the oil over, and bake in the oven for about 15 minutes, until the vegetables are softened and beginning to char.

Meanwhile, cut the baguette into slices and butter them on one side. Cut them in half. Whisk the milk and eggs together in a large bowl. Stir in the grain mustard and about two-thirds of the chopped herbs. Add the bread and the brie to the egg mix and stir everything together. Transfer the mixture to the sheet pan and stir to incorporate the roasted vegetables. Bake for about 40 minutes, until the strata is golden and crisp. Leave to stand for 5 minutes or so. Scatter with the remaining herbs and serve still warm.

SLOW-BAKED ONIONS WITH GOATS' CHEESE, CRISPY BAGUETTE CROUTONS, WALNUTS & BALSAMIC DRESSING

This comforting combination of meltingly soft onions, oozy cheese and crunchy bites of baguette is absolutely top notch. Red onions have a lovely mild flavour when roasted. A rocket/arugula salad is lovely with this.

450 g/1 lb. small red onions, halved
   from root to tip
1 teaspoon fresh thyme leaves
1 tablespoons freshly chopped rosemary
2 teaspoons caster/granulated sugar
4 tablespoons olive oil
1 small baguette
250 g/9 oz. goats' cheese
3 tablespoons walnut pieces
sea salt and freshly ground black pepper

for the dressing
60 ml/¼ cup olive oil
60 ml/¼ cup balsamic vinegar
30 ml/2 tablespoons date syrup
fresh basil leaves, to garnish

SERVES 4

Preheat the oven to 190°C (375°F) Gas 5. Arrange the onion halves over the central area of a large sheet pan. Scatter with the thyme leaves, chopped rosemary and sugar. Season with salt and freshly ground black pepper, drizzle with half of the oil and roast for about 20 minutes, until the onions are starting to soften. Cut the crusts off the baguette (probably nibble on some), and tear the bread into funky-shaped pieces. Toss them with the remaining olive oil and arrange around the edges of the pan. Bake for about 10–15 minutes, until crisp and golden (the onions should still be cooking nicely in the centre). Remove the croutons from the pan and set aside.

Break the goats' cheese up into bite-sized nuggets and scatter over the onions. Toss the walnuts over the top and return to the oven for 5–8 minutes, until the cheese is melting. Spoon the mixture onto a pretty serving plate.

To make the dressing, mix the oil, balsamic vinegar and date syrup together, and season to taste with salt and freshly ground black pepper. Drizzle the dressing over the onions and cheese, scatter with the crispy baguette croutons and garnish with fresh basil leaves. Serve warm.

PAPPA AL POMODORO

225 g/8 oz. good sourdough bread
4–5 tablespoons olive oil
2 garlic cloves, finely chopped
2 x 400-g/14-oz. cans chopped tomatoes
200 g/7 oz. cherry tomatoes
250 ml/1 cup plus 1 tablespoons
   good-quality vegetable stock
1 teaspoon caster/granulated sugar
a handful of roughly torn basil
sea salt and freshly ground black pepper

to serve
2 tablespoons olive oil
fresh basil leaves
50 g/scant 1 cup Parmesan cheese,
   shaved

SERVES 3-4

I fell head over heels with this awesome Italian tomato soup on a week-long press trip to Tuscany. We tucked into a different version every day, often prepared by Tuscan Nonnas, to their secret family recipes. It would definitely be amongst my desert island dishes. This oven-baked version is ace.

Preheat the oven to 190°C (375°F) Gas 5. Tear the bread into pieces and put them into a sheet pan. Add the olive oil and garlic and toss well, until the bread is well coated. Bake for about 10 minutes, until the bread is crisp and golden.

Stir in the canned tomatoes, cherry tomatoes, stock and sugar. Season with salt and freshly ground black pepper. Cover with foil and cook for 20 minutes, until the cherry tomatoes have softened. Remove the foil and crush the cherry tomatoes with the tines of a fork. Stir in the torn basil. Return to the oven for 4–5 minutes more. Drizzle with the oil, scatter with basil leaves and serve with Parmesan shavings.

HARISSA-BAKED AVOCADO, BUTTERNUT SQUASH & EGGS

The addition of spicy harissa to the already colourful flavour and texture combination of green avocado, bright orange butternut squash and eggs, is the ideal way to marry all of these ingredients together. It's rich and tangy in flavour, but the mellowness of the other ingredients contrasts well.

2 tablespoons harissa paste
2 tablespoons olive oil
550 g/1¼ lb. butternut squash, peeled, deseeded and roughly chopped into 2-cm/¾-in. cubes
60 g/½ cup pitted/stoned black olives
15 cherry tomatoes
1 ripe avocado, peeled, pitted/stoned and thinly sliced
freshly squeezed juice of 1 lemon
4 eggs
freshly ground black pepper

SERVES 2

Preheat the oven to 200°C (400°F) Gas 6.

Stir together the harissa paste and olive oil in a large bowl then toss in the butternut squash and stir again to coat the squash.

Put the butternut squash on a sheet pan with sides and bake in the preheated oven for 30 minutes.

Meanwhile, prepare the avocado and squeeze over the lemon juice to prevent it from turning brown. After 30 minutes, add the olives, tomatoes and avocado to the butternut squash and bake for a further 10 minutes.

Make four wells in the vegetables and crack in the eggs. Bake for another 6–9 minutes until the egg whites are cooked. Season with freshly ground black pepper and serve.

BAKED FRITTATA

An extremely versatile dish that allows some flexibility in adding your own leftover vegetables
to the mix, to create a filling egg-based tray bake.

2 large red onions, halved and sliced
10 mushrooms, stalks removed and cut
   into thick slices
1 tablespoon olive oil
8 eggs
2 tablespoons mixed freshly chopped herbs
sea salt and freshly ground black pepper

a 20 x 20-cm/8 x 8-in. sheet pan with sides

SERVES 4

Preheat the oven to 200°C (400°F) Gas 6.

Lay the onion and mushroom slices out on the sheet pan. Drizzle over the
olive oil. Bake in the preheated oven for 15 minutes until soft. Turn the
vegetables over with a spoon once during cooking.

Meanwhile, whisk together the eggs, herbs and seasoning in a large bowl.

When the vegetables are soft, pour the egg mixture over the vegetables
and bake for a further 15 minutes until the egg mix is cooked. Serve.

Serving Suggestion: Serve the frittata in slices with a green salad.

Variation: When you add the egg mix you can also add leftover vegetables
or small tomato halves.

BLACK BEAN NACHOS

A fantastic sharing dish for when you have friends over and you have little time to prepare something.
Watch everyone dig in with delight!

1 x 400-g/14-oz. can black beans, drained
   and rinsed
1 x 230-g/8-oz. pot fresh salsa
½ teaspoon sea salt
100 g/3½ oz. tortilla chips
120 g/1 packed cup plus 3 tablespoons
   grated Cheddar cheese
guacamole, to serve
soured cream, to serve

SERVES 2–4

Preheat the oven to 220°C (425°F) Gas 7.

Combine the black beans, salsa and salt in a food processor to make
a thick paste.

Spread the paste in the base of a sheet pan with sides. Top with the tortilla
chips and then add the cheese.

Bake in the preheated oven for 10 minutes or until the cheese has melted.

Serve immediately with the guacamole and soured cream.

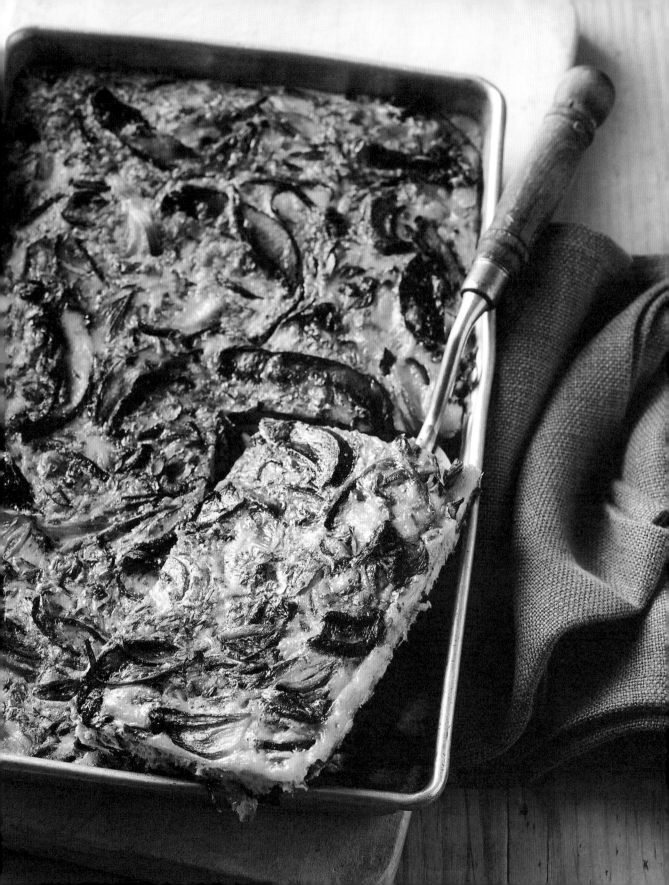

BAKED HONEY & THYME CAMEMBERT WITH CRUDITÉS

How to make friends and influence people? Serve them this oozing, melted cheese with a selection of colourful chopped vegetables and apple slices.

1 x 250-g/9-oz. Camembert
leaves from 2 sprigs of fresh thyme
2 tablespoons runny honey
1 red (bell) pepper, sliced into 1-cm/½-in.
    pieces
1 Granny Smith apple, cored and sliced
    into 8 wedges
1 large carrot, cut into 3-cm/1¼-in. fingers

SERVES 2-4

Preheat the oven to 200°C (400°F) Gas 6.

Score the top of the Camembert with a sharp knife, but leave the cheese in the box.

Push the thyme leaves into the scores, then drizzle over the honey. Replace the lid, loosely, and place the box on a sheet pan.

Bake the Camembert in the preheated oven for 20 minutes until the cheese is all melted and wobbles when you move the sheet pan gently.

Serve the Camembert with the (bell) pepper, apple and carrot crudités.

Serving Suggestion: Serve with chunks of sourdough bread.

BAKED MEDITERRANEAN FETA

Feta has such a unique flavour and texture it deserves to be the star of the show in this 'dish of its own'. This is a very sociable dish.

200 g/7 oz. feta, cut into 4 triangles
2 medium vine tomatoes, quartered
    lengthways
½ courgette/zucchini, thinly sliced
    with a mandolin or peeler
⅛ teaspoon dried basil
⅛ teaspoon dried marjoram
2 tablespoons olive oil
grated zest and freshly squeezed juice
    of ½ lemon

SERVES 2

Preheat the oven to 180°C (350°F) Gas 4.

Place all of the ingredients into a bowl and mix together using your hands. Tip the ingredients onto a small sheet pan with sides.

Bake in the preheated oven for 15 minutes or until the vegetables are cooked. Serve whilst warm.

Serving Suggestion: Serve with avocado slices and a green salad.

GOATS' CHEESE & VEG STACKS

These colourful and nutrient-rich cheese and vegetable stacks are not only mouth-watering but also really simple to create.

2 medium sweet potatoes, peeled and cut into 1-cm/½-in. thick discs
2 medium aubergines/eggplants, cut into 2-cm/¾-in. thick discs
3 tablespoons olive oil
1½ teaspoons sea salt
2 beef tomatoes, cut into 2-cm/¾-in. thick discs

150 g/5½ oz. goats' cheese log, cut into 1-cm/½-in. thick discs
2 teaspoons dried basil
freshly ground black pepper

SERVES 3-4

Preheat the oven to 200°C (400°F) Gas 6.

Lay the sweet potato and aubergine/eggplant discs out on a large sheet pan. Cover in the olive oil (more so on the aubergines/eggplants) and salt and bake in the preheated oven for up to 20 minutes – until they are just cooked.

Once cooked, on the same sheet pan, stack a tomato disc, then the cooked aubergine/eggplant, followed by the cooked sweet potato and finally the goats' cheese.

Bake for another 10 minutes. Sprinkle over the dried basil and freshly ground black pepper and serve.

Serving Suggestion: Serve with a large salad.

COURGETTE CRUST MINI PESTO QUICHES

A light summer supper. These mini quiches are delicious served with a large salad, avocado and coleslaw.

1 courgette/zucchini, very thinly sliced with a mandolin or vegetable peeler (discard the core, it is too wet to use in this recipe)
4 eggs
2 tablespoons green pesto
2 vines of cherry tomatoes
4 x silicone muffin cases, greased, or a muffin pan, greased

SERVES 2

Preheat the oven to 200°C (400°F) Gas 6.

Line the four silicone muffin cases/pan holes, including the base, with one layer of sliced courgette/zucchini. Don't worry if there's some overlap.

Next, whisk together the eggs and pesto in a medium-sized bowl and pour the mixture into the muffin holes.

Bake in the preheated oven for 18–20 minutes until risen and no runny egg remains. Add the tomatoes to the oven 10 minutes before the end of baking (either on the same baking sheet as the muffin cases or a separate sheet if using a muffin pan for the quiches).

Serving Suggestion: Serve the mini quiches and tomatoes together with some sliced avocado and coleslaw.

ROASTED FIG SALAD

Such a wonderful flavour combination – salty blue cheese and sweet figs. Although this is a light meal it is very satisfying. If the rocket/arugula is too peppery for some, then try a little romaine or Little Gem Lettuce underneath the cheesy baked figs.

4 fresh, ripe figs
40 g/1½ oz. blue cheese, crumbled
90 g/3¼ oz. rocket/arugula leaves
35 g/¼ cup chopped walnuts

for the dressing
1¼ teaspoons olive oil
2 teaspoons balsamic vinegar
¼ teaspoon runny honey
¼ teaspoon wholegrain mustard
sea salt and freshly ground black pepper

SERVES 2

Preheat the oven to 200°C (400°F) Gas 6.

Carefully cut halfway down each fig from the top, in a cross. Push the sides of the fig together so that it opens up slightly and put on a sheet pan with sides.

Crumble the blue cheese into the cross of each fig and bake in the preheated oven for 4 minutes.

Meanwhile, make the dressing by whisking together the ingredients in a bowl or shaking in a jar to combine.

Put some rocket/arugula leaves on two plates and top with two of the figs filled with blue cheese, then drizzle some of the dressing. Scatter over the walnuts and serve.

HONEY HARISSA HALLOUMI BAKE

A summery supper that may make you believe that you are indeed on holiday in sunnier climes. The sweet honey and mild spices contrast deliciously with the salty halloumi cheese. One to be eaten whilst hot, otherwise the cheese can turn a little rubbery as it cools.

2 red onions, sliced into wedges
200 g/7 oz. peeled and deseeded butternut squash, cut into 1-cm/½-in. cubes
1 teaspoon olive oil
½ teaspoon sea salt

1 teaspoon harissa dry spice mix
1 teaspoon runny honey
150 g/5½ oz. halloumi, cut into 1-cm/½-in. cubes

SERVES 2

Preheat the oven to 200°C (400°F) Gas 6.

Put the onion and butternut squash on a sheet pan with sides. Drizzle over the olive oil and sprinkle over the salt. Bake in the preheated oven for 30 minutes.

Meanwhile, mix together the harissa spice and honey in a small bowl or ramekin.

After the vegetables have been baking for 30 minutes, add the halloumi and the harissa/honey mix to the sheet pan and give everything a good stir. Bake for a further 10 minutes. Serve.

GRAIN-FREE TOMATO 'SPAGHETTI' BAKE WITH ROQUEFORT

Whilst many have got over their 'spiralizing craze' this dish holds onto the best bit of the phase, which is the fact that spiralized vegetables bake beautifully and quickly, and create a great lower-carb alternative to the classic pasta bake recipe.

175 g/6 oz. courgetti (courgette/zucchini
  thinly sliced using a spiralizer
  or julienne peeler)
175 g/6 oz. butternut squash 'spaghetti'
  (prepared butternut squash sliced
  using a spiralizer or julienne peeler)
1 teaspoon olive oil
1 teaspoon sea salt
2 eggs
330 g/11½ oz. tomato pasta sauce
  (recipe below)
12 pitted black olives
75 g/2¾ oz. crumbled Roquefort

for the sauce
1 teaspoon olive oil
1 onion, chopped
1 courgette/zucchini, chopped
¼ teaspoon garlic salt
½ teaspoon sea salt
1 tablespoon tomato purée/paste
1 x 400-g/14-oz. can chopped tomatoes
1 teaspoon dried oregano

SERVES 4

First, to make the sauce, heat the olive oil in a medium-sized saucepan. Add the onion and cook for 5 minutes until it's beginning to become translucent. Add the courgette/zucchini and cook for a further 5 minutes.

Add the garlic salt, salt, tomato purée/paste, chopped tomatoes and oregano. Cook for 10 minutes.

Pour the sauce mixture into a food processor and process to the consistency of a thick tomato sauce. Transfer to a small saucepan and keep at a gentle simmer over a low heat until ready to use.

Preheat the oven to 200°C (400°F) Gas 6.

Put the courgetti and butternut squash 'spaghetti' in a sheet pan or baking dish with sides. Drizzle over the olive oil and sprinkle on the salt. Mix well. Bake in the preheated oven for 10 minutes.

Meanwhile, whisk the eggs in a large bowl and then add the hot pasta sauce and stir.

Remove the vegetable 'spaghetti' from the oven, then pour over the sauce mixture. Any remaining sauce can be kept in the fridge for up to 3 days. Add the olives and crumbled Roquefort before serving. Place the dish under a medium grill/broiler to melt the cheese, if desired, and serve.

POTATO & ROSEMARY PIZZA

This pizza is vegan-friendly, made from the kind of staples you generally have in the house – and if you use fast-action yeast, it's doesn't take too long from start to finish either. Simplicity at its winning best. If possible, cut and soak the potato slices in cold water for 30 minutes or so before making the pizza bases. This helps the potatoes crisp more efficiently.

for the pizza base
500 g/3½–3⅔ cups strong plain bread flour
1 teaspoon fine sea salt
1 teaspoon caster/granulated sugar
7 g/¼ oz. sachet fast-action dried yeast
1 tablespoon olive oil
about 300 ml/1¼ cups hand-hot water

for the topping
600 g/21 oz. smallish floury potatoes, soaked
  and very thinly sliced (as intro)
4 tablespoon olive oil
2 tablespoon finely chopped rosemary
a large bunch of spring onions/
  scallions, chopped
sea salt and freshly ground black pepper

SERVES 4

Preheat the oven to 200°C (400°F) Gas 6. Put the flour into a large bowl and stir in the salt and sugar. Add the yeast and mix well. Pour in the olive oil, and add enough hand-hot water to bring the mixture together into a soft, but not sticky dough. Knead the dough for 5–10 minutes, until smooth. Divide the dough into two and roll each piece into a rectangle to fit the base of two sheet pans.

Drain the water from the potatoes and rinse them under running cold water one final time. Dry thoroughly on paper towels or a clean kitchen towel. Toss them into a large bowl with the olive oil, rosemary and a generous sprinkling of salt flakes and black pepper, until all the slices are evenly coated.Scatter the spring onions/scallions between the two bases. Top with the potato slices, overlapping the potato edges very slightly, until the bases are covered. Bake the pizzas for about 20 minutes or so, until the potatoes are cooked and crispy golden at the edges.

Cut into squares and serve at once.

OVEN-BAKED BUTTERNUT SQUASH, SAFFRON & ROSEMARY RISOTTO

4 g/⅛ oz. saffron filaments
1 onion, chopped
25 g/1½ tablespoons butter
2 tablespoons olive oil
400 g/14 oz. peeled, deseeded butternut
  squash, cut into bite-sized cubes
300 g/1⅔ cups carnaroli rice
120 ml/½ cup dry white wine
800 ml/generous 3¼ cups well-flavoured
  vegetable stock
1 tablespoon freshly chopped rosemary

for the mantecatura
50 g/3½ tablespoons butter
80 g/1¼ cups Parmesan cheese, grated

SERVES 4

Having had a house in Italy for 10 years, I do have a soft spot for a good risotto. Purists may tut-tut at the idea of making one in the oven, but it does work surprisingly well – just keep an eye on timing, so that the rice doesn't overcook.

Preheat the oven to 200°C (400°F) Gas 6. Put the saffron filaments into a small bowl and pour on a couple of tablespoons of just-boiled water. Leave to infuse. Scatter the chopped onion over the base of a deep sheet pan. Add the butter and olive oil. Transfer to the oven for 10 minutes, until the onion is starting to soften.

Add the butternut squash to the sheet pan. Stir in the rice, until everything is coated with the oil and butter. Pour in the wine, stock and saffron and stir in the rosemary. Cover the pan with foil and return to the oven. Cook for about 20 minutes or so, until the rice is cooked but still has a little bite. Remove from the oven, stir in the butter and Parmesan for the mantecatura and serve.

CARROT TART TATIN SQUARES WITH GINGER & MINT YOGURT

1.5 kg/3 lb. 5 oz. carrots
250 g/9 oz. shallots, peeled
3 tablespoons honey
2 tablespoons olive oil
1 tablespoon fresh thyme leaves
30 g/2 tablespoons butter, softened
3 tablespoons light brown
  muscovado sugar
300 g/10½ oz. ready-made puff pastry
sea salt and freshly ground black pepper

for the yogurt
200 g/scant 1 cup natural/plain full
  fat yogurt
2 cm/¾ inch fresh piece of ginger root,
  finely grated
1 garlic clove, grated
a small bunch of mint leaves, roughly torn
extra mint, to garnish

a 30 x 17 x 2.5 cm/11¾ x 6¾ x 1 inch
  brownie pan

MAKES 12 SQUARES

When you put glossy, caramelized carrots, soft candied shallots and crisp flaky pastry together, you really can't fail to end up with something very special, and this tatin is certainly that.

Preheat the oven to 190°C (375°F) Gas 5. Cut the carrots into triangular chunks about 2 cm/¾ inch wide at the base. Scatter them over the base of a sheet pan and add the peeled shallots. Mix the honey, olive oil and thyme leaves together and then spoon the mixture over the vegetables. Season and roast for about 30 minutes, until the carrots have started to soften. Remove the pan from the oven and stir in the butter and muscovado sugar.

Roll the pastry out to fit the pan and place it carefully over the vegetables, tucking the edges in. Bake for about 25 minutes or so, until the pastry is golden and crisp. Remove from the oven and leave to settle for 4–5 minutes, before turning out and inverting onto a board and cutting into squares.

Stir the yogurt, grated ginger and grated garlic together in a bowl. Add the torn mint leaves and season with a little salt and freshly ground black pepper. Arrange the carrot tatin squares on a pretty serving dish and garnish with extra mint leaves. Serve the yogurt in a bowl alongside.

ROAST MINI PEPPERS WITH FETA, OLIVES & PESTO

400 g/14 oz. mini (bell) peppers, halved
  and deseeded
250 g/9 oz. cherry tomatoes, quartered
2 garlic cloves, finely chopped
4 tablespoons olive oil
100 g/1 cup pitted black olives
200 g/7 oz. feta cheese
sea salt and freshly ground black pepper

for the pesto
80 ml/⅓ cup olive oil
2 garlic cloves, chopped
80 g/1¼ cups Parmesan cheese, grated
40 g/⅓ cup pine nuts/kernals
2 big handfuls of fresh basil leaves

SERVES 4

If you want to make this dish plant-based only, substitute a vegan cheese or serve everything without cheese, but add the juice of a lemon to the oil, basil and garlic, replacing the more traditional pesto with a dressing.

Preheat the oven to 190°C (375°F) Gas 5. Arrange the mini peppers on a large, flat sheet pan and the tomatoes over the top. Sprinkle the chopped garlic over, and then drizzle with olive oil. Season and roast for about 20–25 minutes, until the peppers are soft and starting to char a little at the edges.

Remove the sheet pan from the oven and scatter over the olives. Break the feta into nuggets and scatter them over everything.

For the pesto, put the olive oil, garlic cloves, grated Parmesan and pine nuts into a small food processor (or you could use a jug/pitcher and stick blender). Add the basil leaves and whiz until you have a lightly textured but evenly mixed paste. Season, then dot small spoonfuls of the pesto here and there over the peppers, olives and feta. Serve warm or at room temperature.

GREEK POTATO & COURGETTE BAKE WITH FETA & FRESH HERBS

This garlic and herb-flecked combination of courgettes, tomatoes and potatoes is the vegetable equivalent of a 'super-group' – what an astoundingly harmonious merger they make. The potatoes are briefly soaked in water, and then rinsed to help remove some of the starch. Don't be tempted to skip on the rinsing. If you merely tip them into a colander or sieve to drain them, you will be flushing all the starchy water back over them, and this will defeat the object of soaking them.

800 g/28 oz. floury potatoes, peeled and
   cut into 3 mm/⅛ inch slices
5 ripe tomatoes, roughly chopped
2 fairly large courgettes/zucchinis,
   thinly sliced
4–5 tablespoons olive oil
2 garlic cloves, chopped
1 tablespoon dried oregano
200 g/7 oz. feta cheese, cut into
   bite-sized chunks
a small bunch of parsley, roughly chopped
sea salt and freshly ground black pepper

SERVES 4

Preheat the oven to 190°C (375°F) Gas 5. Put the potato slices into a large bowl, cover them with cold water and leave them to soak for 10 minutes. Pour them into a colander or large sieve/strainer and rinse them under the cold water tap, until the water runs clear. Dry them on paper towels. Rinse and dry the bowl and return the dried potato slices to it. Add the chopped tomatoes and sliced courgettes/zucchinis. Pour in the olive oil and stir in the chopped garlic and oregano. Season with salt and freshly ground black pepper. Spread the vegetables over a deep sheet pan and cook for about 1 hour, until everything is golden and the potatoes are crisp.

Remove the pan from the oven. Scatter the feta over the vegetables. Sprinkle over the chopped parsley and serve at once.

BAY-SCENTED SUMMER VEGETABLE TIAN

This dish is so simple to make and absolutely sings of summer when it comes out of the oven, bubbling and golden, scenting the air with a gorgeous, aromatic waft of bay. It's a real people-pleaser, and could even be adapted for a vegan diet if the mozzarella was replaced with one of the plant-based cheese substitutes that are readily available now.

2 courgettes/zucchinis, sliced
6 ripe tomatoes, sliced
350 g/12 oz. potatoes, very thinly sliced
80 ml/⅓ cup olive oil
1 teaspoon oregano
2 teaspoons fresh thyme leaves
350 g/12 oz. mozzarella, sliced
2 small leeks, trimmed and sliced
4–5 fresh bay leaves
sea salt and freshly ground black pepper

a 30 x 17 x 2.5 cm/11¾ x 6¾ x 1 inch
   brownie pan, lightly greased

SERVES 4

Preheat the oven to 190°C (375°F) Gas 5. Put the courgette/zucchini and tomato slices into a large bowl together. Put the potatoes slices into a large sieve, or colander. Rinse the potatoes for a minute or so under the cold water tap, to remove as much starch as possible, then put them into a separate bowl. Divide all but a tablespoon or two of the olive oil between the two bowls, and toss the vegetables to thoroughly coat them, then season each with salt and freshly ground black pepper and add the oregano and thyme leaves.

Arrange the vegetables and mozzarella in alternating layers across a sheet pan, standing the slices up on their edges, and packing them quite tightly. Scatter in the sliced leeks as you go. Cut the bay leaves in half and tuck them in here and there. Drizzle over the remaining oil, transfer the sheet pan to the oven and bake for about 50 minutes or so, until the vegetables are cooked and golden. Remove the bay leaves and serve.

VEGAN

CRUSHED BUTTER BEANS WITH ROASTED TOMATOES & AVOCADO

This dish is fabulous with crusty bread or sourdough toast for scooping up, and far better than any beans on toast you've ever tasted! I think it makes a perfect brunch dish, and an easy way to feed friends or family when you fancy something hot and tasty. It's a favourite of mine for lunch too.

600 g/21 oz. cherry tomatoes
4 tablespoons olive oil
3–4 leeks, trimmed and sliced
1 garlic clove, finely chopped
1 x 400-g/14-oz. can butter/lima beans, drained and rinsed
a bunch of parsley, coarsely chopped
2 ripe, but firm avocados
chilli/chile oil (optional)
paprika, to sprinkle
parsley leaves, to garnish

SERVES 4

Preheat the oven to 180°C (350°F) Gas 4.

Scatter the cherry tomatoes over a large sheet pan and drizzle the olive oil over. Add the leeks and garlic and toss everything together. Roast for 20 minutes. Remove the sheet pan from the oven and scatter the butter/ lima beans evenly over the tomatoes. Crush the beans lightly using the tines of a fork. Scatter over the chopped parsley. Return the sheet pan to the oven for a further 5 minutes.

Remove from the oven. Cut the avocados in half, remove the pits and scoop out the flesh using a teaspoon. Arranged evenly over the beans and tomatoes. Drizzle with chilli/chile oil (if using), add a light sprinkling of paprika and garnish with parsley leaves.

TURMERIC TOFU & ROASTED VEGGIE SCRAMBLE

Roasted vegetables and scrambled tofu make an incredibly pleasing partnership. Here's another one you'll want to get the gloves out for – yellow stained hands aren't a particularly fetching look, and fresh turmeric does tend to leave its mark that way.

1 onion, chopped
1 red (bell) pepper, deseeded and diced
1 orange (bell) pepper, deseeded and diced
200 g/7 oz. cherry tomatoes, halved
100 g/3½ oz. chestnut mushrooms
6 tablespoons olive oil
250 g/9 oz. firm tofu
20 g/¾ oz. fresh turmeric, peeled and finely grated
1 tablespoon dark soy sauce
a bunch of freshly chopped parsley
sea salt and freshly ground black pepper
chilli/chile oil, to serve

SERVES 4

Preheat the oven to 190°C (375°F) Gas 5.

Scatter the onion over a large, flat sheet pan. Scatter the (bell) peppers over the onion. Cut the tomatoes in half and scatter these over the onion and (bell) peppers. Slice the mushrooms and add them to the pan. Drizzle with all but 1 tablespoon of the olive oil and roast for about 10 minutes until the vegetables are soft and lightly charred.

Mash the tofu in a large bowl with the remaining tablespoon of oil, the turmeric and soy sauce. Season with salt and pepper and add to the roasted vegetables and stir to combine. Return to the oven for 5 minutes, until everything is hot. Scatter with chopped parsley, and serve with chilli/chile oil.

PESTO-BAKED MUSHROOMS WITH SUN-DRIED TOMATOES

A delightful summery vegan dish with meltingly soft mushrooms combined with the classic flavours of pesto, tomatoes and capers. Of course, cooked mushrooms provide an 'umami' taste that is ever so satisfying.

4 large flat mushrooms
4 heaped teaspoons vegan pesto
   (recipe below)
3 tablespoons sun-dried tomatoes
   in olive oil, drained
1 tablespoon capers or 2 tablespoons
   black olives
olive oil, for drizzling

SERVES 4
AS A STARTER

Preheat the oven to 180°C (350°F) Gas 4.

Wipe the mushrooms clean and remove the stalks. Spread the pesto onto the underside of the mushrooms with the back of a teaspoon. Place the mushrooms on a sheet pan with sides and bake in the preheated oven for 15 minutes.

Add the capers or olives and sun-dried tomatoes to the sheet pan and cook for a further 7–10 minutes until everything is the same temperature. Remove from the oven and serve.

VEGAN PESTO

Pesto is surprisingly simple to prepare and can really elevate a dish. It's delicious paired with baked mushrooms, courgettes and kale.

40 g/¼ cup sunflower seeds
75 g/5 cups fresh basil leaves
½ garlic clove, peeled
1 teaspoon freshly squeezed lemon juice
5 tablespoons olive oil
sea salt and freshly ground black pepper

To make the pesto, put the sunflower seeds into a food processor and whizz to a powder. Add all the other ingredients (except the oil) and whizz until combined. Finally, add the oil, whizz to mix and check the seasoning.

The pesto can be stored in a glass jar with a lid for up to 3 days in the refrigerator.

PESTO SUMMER VEG BAKE

Pesto IS the taste of summer and especially when combined with seasonal vegetables
as it is in this perfect summer dish.

2 medium courgettes/zucchini, sliced into
   3-mm/⅛-in. thick rounds
1 medium aubergine/eggplant, sliced into
   3-mm/⅛-in. thick rounds
12 cherry tomatoes
4 tablespoons Vegan Pesto (page 106)
4 tablespoons olive oil
1 tablespoon freshly chopped parsley

SERVES 4

Preheat the oven to 180°C (350°F) Gas 4.

Place all of the vegetables in a bowl. Mix together the pesto and olive oil
to create pesto oil. Pour over the vegetables and stir to coat them.

Lay all the vegetables out on two sheet pans with sides. Bake them in the
preheated oven for 30 minutes, turning them over from time to time.

Scatter the parsley over the top before serving.

Serving Suggestion: Layer the vegetables together in a serving dish and
serve with a green salad.

VEGETABLE RISOTTO

The joy of not having to stand over the hob stirring constantly and still getting a perfectly textured
risotto after 45 minutes baking! There's versatility in this recipe and scope to make it your own
by roasting your own vegetables or adding your own leftover vegetables too.

1 red onion, sliced into wedges (roughly
   8 wedges)
10 mushrooms, cut into quarters
1 red (bell) pepper, deseeded and cut
   into thin slices
1 tablespoon olive oil
¼ teaspoon sea salt
200 g/1 cup Arborio rice
400 ml/1⅔ cups hot vegetable stock
1 tablespoon nutritional yeast flakes
   (optional)
1 tablespoon freshly chopped flat leaf parsley
sea salt and freshly ground black pepper

SERVES 4

Preheat the oven to 200°C (400°F) Gas 6.

Put the vegetables in a medium-sized sheet pan with sides, drizzle over
the olive oil and sprinkle over the salt. Bake in the preheated oven for
15 minutes.

Add the rice and stir. Add the vegetable stock, then cover the sheet pan
tightly with foil. Bake in the oven for a further 30 minutes.

Stir in the yeast flakes, if using. Season to taste. Scatter the parsley over
the top and serve.

Serving Suggestion: Serve with avocado and rocket/arugula salad, drizzled
with olive oil and freshly squeezed lemon juice, plus a little black pepper.

SWEET POTATO FALAFEL WITH COURGETTES & PEPPERS

This dish, incorporating flavour-packed falafel with roasted courgettes/zucchini and (bell) peppers, is a favourite with all ages from babies, who can enjoy it as finger food, to older folk.

1 courgette/zucchini, cut into 2-cm/¾-in. thick rounds
1 red (bell) pepper, deseeded and cut into 2-cm/¾-in. thick strips
2 teaspoons olive oil
sea salt and freshly ground black pepper

for the falafel
400 g/14 oz. cooked sweet potatoes (skins removed)
100 g/¾ cup canned chickpeas, drained and rinsed
50 g/⅓ cup gram (chickpea) flour
½ teaspoon ground coriander
1 teaspoon ground cumin
freshly squeezed juice of ¼ lemon
½ teaspoon sea salt

SERVES 4

Put all the falafel ingredients into a food processor and whizz to combine to a smooth but thick paste. Transfer to a bowl, cover and leave in the refrigerator for 24 hours.

Preheat the oven to 190°C (375°F) Gas 5.

Remove the falafel mixture from the refrigerator and shape into small falafel quenelles using two spoons.

Put the falafel, courgette/zucchini and (bell) pepper on a sheet pan with sides and sprinkle over the olive oil and seasoning.

Bake in the preheated oven for 25 minutes.

Serve the falafel and baked vegetables together and enjoy.

SAFFRON CAULIFLOWER STEAKS WITH CANDIED JERUSALEM ARTICHOKES, ROASTED GRAPES, PISTACHIOS & LIME CHERMOULA

Thick slices of cauliflower look so pretty and taste so good when they're given a slick of saffron-infused oil and cooked in the oven. If you've never roasted grapes before, then I think you'll be won over when you try them – especially in this dish, where they perfectly complement the other elements and are set off beautifully with a piquant lime chermoula dressing.

a generous pinch of saffron filaments
juice of 1 lemon
500 g/18 oz. Jerusalem artichokes
1 large cauliflower
50 ml/3½ tablespoons olive oil
1 scant teaspoon paprika
20 g/¾ oz. light brown muscovado sugar
300 g/2 cups small, sweet juicy red grapes
50 g/1¾ oz. pistachios

for the lime chermoula
80 ml/⅓ cup extra virgin olive oil
2 garlic cloves, chopped
1 teaspoon cumin seeds
1 teaspoon ground coriander
1 teaspoon dried chilli/red pepper flakes
a large bunch of coriander/cilantro, coarsely chopped
a large bunch of parsley, coarsely chopped
a small handful of mint leaves
zest and juice of 1 large lime

SERVES 4

Preheat the oven to 190°C (375°F) Gas 5.

Put the saffron filaments into a small bowl and stir in a tablespoon of just-boiled water. Set aside.

Fill a large bowl with cold water and add the lemon juice. Peel the artichokes, cut into slices, then drop them into the acidulated water to prevent them from browning.

Cut the cauliflower into thick slices to form 'steaks'. Transfer the cauliflower slices to a large, flat sheet pan. Stir 30 ml/2 tablespoons of the olive oil into the saffron infusion and drizzle this over the cauliflower. Sprinkle the slices with the paprika.

Mix the remaining olive oil with the muscovado sugar. Remove the artichoke slices from the acidulated water and dry briefly on paper towels. Toss them with the oil and sugar mixture. Scatter them over the sheet pan and transfer to the oven. Roast for about 15 minutes, until the vegetables are almost soft.

Cut the grapes into small clusters and arrange them over the pan. Return the pan to the oven and cook for another 10–15 minutes, until the vegetables are soft and golden, and the grape skins are starting to split a little and caramelize. Remove the sheet pan from the oven and scatter over pistachios.

To make the lime chermoula, simply put all the ingredients into a food processor and blitz to a fairly smooth sauce. Drizzle over the cauliflower steaks, and serve.

CHICKPEA & ALMOND CURRY

This makes a fabulous, reasonably inexpensive but very healthy weekday supper and is equally suitable for both vegetarians and anyone following a plant-based diet.

2 onions, sliced
4–5 tablespoons olive oil
2 teaspoons garam masala
1 teaspoon ground turmeric
1 teaspoon ground coriander
1 teaspoon ground cumin
1 teaspoon dried chilli/red
 pepper flakes
60 g/2¼ oz. fresh ginger
2 garlic cloves, finely chopped
2 x 400-g/14-oz. cans
 chopped tomatoes

2 x 400-g/14-oz. cans
 chickpeas, drained and
 rinsed
2 tablespoons good-quality
 tomato ketchup
80 g/¾ cup ground almonds
freshly chopped coriander/
 cilantro leaves
1 red chilli/chile, deseeded
 and sliced, to garnish

SERVES 4

Preheat the oven to 190°C (375°F) Gas 5. Scatter the onion slices over the base of a deep sheet pan and drizzle with the olive oil. Add the garam masala, turmeric, ground coriander, cumin and chilli/red pepper flakes. Stir to coat the onions in the spices. Roast for 10 minutes.

Peel the ginger and cut it into julienne. Remove the pan from the oven and add the ginger and chopped garlic. Stir in the chopped tomatoes, chickpeas, tomato ketchup and ground almonds. Return the pan to the oven and cook for about 20–25 minutes, until the sauce is lovely and thickened. Garnish with chopped coriander/cilantro and red chilli/chile slices.

EASY OVEN DAL

This comforting dal is quick and easy to make and cooks beautifully by itself in the oven. If you're like me and tend to have some fresh ginger in the fridge, canned tomatoes in the cupboard, and have a few basic spices – then it's a real storecupboard supper. I like it with a scattering of extra chilli/red pepper flakes and a slick of yogurt, but if you prefer to make it dairy-free, then some fruity chutney makes a great match too.

1 onion, sliced
5 tablespoons olive oil
1 teaspoon ground cumin
1 teaspoon ground coriander
1 teaspoon ground turmeric
60 g/2¼ oz. fresh ginger
1 teaspoon dried chilli/red
 pepper flakes (or to taste)
1 teaspoon caster/
 granulated sugar
2 garlic cloves, chopped
300 g/1¾ cups dried red
 lentils, rinsed

800 ml/generous 3¼ cups
 water
1 x 400-g/14-oz. can
 chopped tomatoes
sea salt flakes and freshly
 ground black pepper
extra chilli/red pepper flakes,
 natural/plain vegan yogurt,
 and/or chutney, to serve

SERVES 4

Preheat the oven to 190°C (375°F) Gas 5. Scatter the onion over the base of a deep sheet pan. Drizzle the olive oil over and stir in the cumin, coriander and turmeric. Transfer to the oven and cook for 10 minutes.

In the meantime, peel the ginger and cut it into julienne. Remove the sheet pan from the oven and stir in the ginger julienne, the chilli/red pepper flakes, sugar and chopped garlic. Stir in the red lentils, water and canned tomatoes. Cover the sheet pan with foil, and cook for about 30–35 minutes, until the lentils are soft and the dal has a nice creamy texture (you may have to add a little more water if it seems to be getting a little too dry). Season with salt flakes and freshly ground black pepper, and serve with extra chilli/red pepper flakes and vegan yogurt or chutney (or both!).

FRESH LIME, VEGETABLE & COCONUT CURRY

I love Thai coconut curries, but more often than not, standard Thai curry pastes usually contain dried shrimps or fish sauce – so I've come up with this delicious and easily made alternative paste. It helps if you have a food processor, or mini chopper, but you could also make the paste using a pestle and mortar. The vegetables don't need to be cooked for too long, otherwise they will lose their lovely vibrant colour and crispy texture. If you're using long-stemmed broccoli, opt for young, smaller stems.

for the curry paste
45 g/1½ oz. knob of fresh ginger, peeled
2 garlic cloves, peeled
1 stalk lemongrass, trimmed
3 mukrat lime leaves
1 tablespoon ground coriander
1 tablespoon ground cumin
1 scant tablespoon dried chilli/red pepper flakes
1 tablespoon coconut oil
1–2 tablespoons warm water
a bunch of fresh coriander/cilantro

for the curry
2 x 400-ml/14-fl. oz. cans full fat coconut milk
100 ml/⅓ cup plus 1 tablespoon well-flavoured vegetable stock
1 tablespoon demerara/turbinado sugar
100 g/3½ oz. cherry tomatoes, roughly chopped
1 yellow (bell) pepper, deseeded and cut into strips
400 g/14 oz. mixed young vegetables (sugar snap peas, green/French beans, young, long-stem broccoli, baby sweetcorn, etc.)
a small bunch of fresh coriander/cilantro, roughly chopped
zest and juice of 1 large lime

to serve
a handful of cashew nuts
a bunch of spring onions/scallions, thinly sliced

SERVES 4

To make the curry paste, roughly chop the ginger, garlic and lemongrass and add them to a food processor or mini chopper and whiz until finely chopped (or bash them using a pestle and mortar if preferred). Add the lime leaves, ground coriander, cumin, chilli/red pepper flakes and coconut oil. Pour in the warm water and blitz everything to a paste. Add the coriander/cilantro and whiz again until everything is ground down and evenly mixed.

Preheat the oven to 180°C (350°F) Gas 4.

For the curry, pour the coconut milk and stock into a deep roasting pan and stir in the curry paste and sugar. Cover with foil and cook for 15 minutes. Remove the roasting pan from the oven, give everything a good stir and add the chopped tomatoes, (bell) pepper strips and prepared vegetables (cut the baby/sweet corn in half from top to bottom, if using). Replace the foil and cook for 10 minutes, until the vegetables are just soft but retain their bright colours. Stir in the fresh coriander/cilantro and add the lime zest and juice. Serve straight away, scattered with cashews and spring onions/scallions.

TURMERIC MACADAMIAS

Macadamia nuts have a beautiful, buttery texture. When they're roasted with a light scattering of turmeric, they become absolutely irresistible. I find it very easy to polish off a whole batch this size on my own.

150 g/5½ oz. macadamias
1 tablespoon olive oil
1 teaspoon ground turmeric
1 teaspoon brown rice syrup
sea salt flakes

SERVES 2-3

Preheat the oven to 190°C (375°F) Gas 5.

Put the macadamias into a large bowl and add the olive oil, turmeric and brown rice syrup. Season with some salt flakes. Bake for about 4–5 minutes, until golden and roasted. Store well away from temptation.

BUTTERNUT SQUASH & CAULIFLOWER LENTIL KORMA

This is a very cost-effective and colourful vegan tray bake, combining sweet but not too starchy butternut squash and cauliflower with lentils and spices. This is a mild vegan curry that will tempt reluctant vegans!

2 red onions, cut into quarters
400 g/14 oz. butternut squash, peeled, deseeded and cut into 1-cm/½-in. cubes
½ cauliflower, cut into florets
2 teaspoons olive oil
60 g/¼ cup korma curry paste
200 ml/generous ¾ cup coconut milk
1 x 400-g/14-oz. can green lentils, drained and rinsed
1 lemon, cut into quarters, to serve
1 tablespoon freshly chopped coriander/ cilantro, to serve

SERVES 2

Preheat the oven to 200°C (400°F) Gas 6.

Put the onions, butternut squash and cauliflower in a sheet pan with sides and drizzle over the olive oil.

Bake in the preheated oven for 30–35 minutes until all the vegetables are soft and the cauliflower is also brown and crispy at the edges.

Meanwhile, mix the curry paste and coconut milk together. Pour the mixture over the vegetables and stir in the lentils.

Bake for a further 10 minutes. Squeeze over the lemon quarters, sprinkle over the coriander/cilantro and serve.

Serving Suggestion: Serve with rice.

VEGAN BAKED FAJITAS

Fajitas seem like the best party food to serve to a crowd. Making up your own fajita whilst sat around a table with your friends or family is such a sociable way to enjoy a meal. In this book, you'll find both meat and vegan fajita dishes so there is something for everyone at party time!

2 medium sweet potatoes, peeled and
  chopped into 1.5-cm/½-in. pieces
3 teaspoons olive oil
2 (bell) peppers, ideally different colours,
  deseeded and cut into 2-cm/¾-in.
  long slices
2 red onions, sliced into thin wedges
1 x 28-g/1-oz. packet of fajita seasoning
  mix (try to avoid those with sugar
  as the prime ingredient)
1 x 400-g/14-oz. can chickpeas, drained
  and rinsed

SERVES 4

Preheat the oven to 200°C (400°F) Gas 6.

Put the sweet potatoes on a large sheet pan with sides. Drizzle over ½ teaspoon of the olive oil. Bake in the preheated oven for 15 minutes.

Meanwhile, mix the (bell) peppers, onions, remaining 2½ teaspoons olive oil and the fajita seasoning together in a bowl.

Once the sweet potatoes have been baking for 15 minutes, add the (bell) pepper and onion mix to the sheet pan and stir.

Bake for another 15 minutes then add the chickpeas for the last minute and stir well. Serve.

Serving Suggestion: Serve with coconut yogurt and either wraps or rice.

BALSAMIC TEMPEH & CRISPY CAULIFLOWER

What a treat tempeh is! A naturally-fermented food which means it is more nutritious and easier to digest than modified and processed soy-based foods. This balsamic tempeh is rich in flavour. Just try it and I bet you'll be coming back for more.

2 tablespoons balsamic glaze
¼ teaspoon garlic salt
1 teaspoon maple syrup
2 tablespoons olive oil
1 x 200-g/7-oz. pack tempeh
½ cauliflower, cut into florets
½ teaspoon sea salt

SERVES 2

Preheat the oven to 190°C (375°F) Gas 5.

In a bowl, mix together the balsamic glaze, garlic salt, maple syrup and 1 tablespoon of the olive oil.

Wash the tempeh and pat it dry. Cut it into 16 squares or triangles.

Place the tempeh into the marinade and turn to coat.

Put the cauliflower florets on a sheet pan with sides, sprinkle over the remaining 1 tablespoon olive oil and the salt. Make a space in the middle of the cauliflower for the tempeh. Tip the tempeh and marinade into the sheet pan.

Roast in the preheated oven for 30–35 minutes until the cauliflower is crispy at the edges and the marinade mostly absorbed. Serve immediately.

HASSELBACK COQUINA SQUASH WITH CHILLI MAPLE GLAZE & SALT FLAKES

You may well have made hasselback potatoes – the gorgeous potatoes that are cooked whole, but thinly sliced along their length almost all the way through, so that the slices fan out slightly as they cook and become crisp and golden. Here, I've used the same method to cook coquina squash (a close relative of the butternut) and glazed it with a sticky-sweet-slightly-spicy combination of maple syrup, soy sauce and chilli/chile. A great trick for cutting the thin slices without inadvertently cutting all the way through, is to lay a chopstick along both lengths of the squash, so that the knife will go no further once it reaches the sticks.

1 coquina squash
50 ml/3½ tablespoon maple syrup
20 ml/4 teaspoon Indonesian soy sauce (ketjap manis)
25 ml/5 teaspoon dark soy sauce
1 teaspoon dried chilli/red pepper flakes
a bunch of spring onions/scallions, diagonally sliced
a handful of fresh coriander/cilantro, roughly chopped

SERVES 3-4

Preheat the oven to 190°C (375°F) Gas 5.

Cut the squash in half from base to top, and scoop out the seeds. Remove the peel using a vegetable peeler. Cut each half widthways into thin slices, stopping a little way short of cutting all the way through so that the squash halves are still intact. Lay them on a lightly oiled sheet pan. Mix the maple syrup, soy sauces and chilli/red pepper flakes together and brush generously over the squash halves, making sure to get plenty in between each slice. Bake for about 30–35 minutes, basting regularly, until the squash is cooked through and has a beautiful shiny glaze.

Transfer to a platter and scatter over the spring onions/scallions and coriander/cilantro. Serve hot.

RATATOUILLE BAKED BEANS

1 medium aubergine/eggplant, cut into
  2-cm/¾-in. cubes
1 red (bell) pepper, deseeded and cut into
  2-cm/¾-in. pieces
¼ large butternut squash, deseeded, peeled
  and cut into 2-cm/¾-in. cubes
1 onion, cut into 8 wedges
1 tablespoon olive oil
1 teaspoon sea salt
1 x 400-g/14-oz. can cannellini beans,
  drained and rinsed
12 stoned/pitted black olives, halved
1 x 400-g/14-oz. can chopped tomatoes
2 tablespoons tomato purée/paste
1 teaspoon maple syrup
1½ teaspoons freshly chopped basil leaves

SERVES 4

A combination of two classics – ratatouille and baked beans – this dish
is delightfully flavoursome. This is an ideal celebratory vegan meal to enjoy
with friends or family.

Preheat the oven to 200°C (400°F) Gas 6.

Place the chopped aubergine/eggplant, (bell) pepper, squash and onion
on a sheet pan with sides. Drizzle over the olive oil and sprinkle over the salt.
Bake in the preheated oven for 30 minutes until the vegetables are soft.

Add the cannellini beans, black olives, chopped tomatoes, tomato purée/paste
and maple syrup and stir. Bake for a further 10 minutes. Serve with the basil
scattered over the top.

Serving Suggestion: Serve with crushed new potatoes.

BLACK BEAN & SWEET POTATO CHILLI

2 large sweet potatoes, peeled and cut into
  2-cm/¾-in. pieces
1 teaspoon coconut or olive oil
1 teaspoon sea salt
2 red onions, cut into 6 wedges
1 red (bell) pepper, halved, deseeded and
  sliced into 1-cm/½-in. thick lengths
1 x 500-g/17-oz. carton passata/strained
  tomatoes
¾ teaspoon smoked paprika
½ teaspoon ground cumin
¾ teaspoon dried marjoram
⅛ teaspoon chilli/chili powder
⅛ teaspoon ground cinnamon
1 x 400-g/14-oz. can black beans, drained
  and rinsed

SERVES 6

This dish provides a rich combination of sweet potatoes with tangy tomatoes
and soft, smooth and satisfying black beans. It's a colourful combination and
ideal for a vegan feast of any proportion.

Preheat the oven to 200°C (400°F) Gas 6.

Put the sweet potatoes in a sheet pan with sides. Drizzle over the melted
coconut oil or olive oil and sprinkle over ¼ teaspoon of the salt. Bake in the
preheated oven for 10 minutes. Add the onions and red (bell) pepper and
bake for a further 20 minutes, stirring once during baking.

Next, mix together the passata/strained tomatoes, paprika, cumin, marjoram,
chilli/chili powder, cinnamon and the remaining ¾ teaspoon salt.

After the vegetables have been baking for 30 minutes, add the black beans
to the sheet pan, stir, then add the passata/strained tomatoes and spice mix.
Stir this well too. Bake for a further 15 minutes, then serve.

ROASTED PEPPER, SWEETCORN & BLACK-EYED BEAN WRAPS WITH CHIPOTLE DRESSING & AVOCADO SPREAD

I have the most gargantuan soft spot for sunny coloured roasted (bell) peppers. They morph into the juiciest, sweetest delights and make a fantastic filling for these moreish tortilla wraps, when partnered with sweet, crunchy corn, black eyed beans and ripe avocado. They're nice with Oven-Roasted Chilli Jam (page 156).

2 red (bell) peppers, deseeded and cut into strips
2 orange (bell) peppers, deseeded and cut into strips
3 tablespoons olive oil
2 corn on the cob/ears of corn
1 x 400-g/14-oz. can black eyed beans
2 ripe avocados, peeled and pitted
juice of 1 lime
1 small red chilli/chile, deseeded and finely chopped
4 flour tortillas

a large bunch of spring onions/scallions, sliced
a small bunch of coriander/cilantro
sea salt and freshly ground black pepper
vegan soured/sour cream, to serve

for the dressing
2 tablespoons chipotle paste
2 tablespoons olive oil
1 tablespoons red wine vinegar
2 teaspoons caster/granulated sugar

SERVES 4

Preheat the oven to 190°C (375°F) Gas 5. Scatter the (bell) peppers over a sheet pan, drizzle over the oil and roast for 15 minutes, until they are starting to soften and char. Cut the kernels from the sweetcorn/corn cobs, add them to the pan with the pepper strips and cook for a further 10 minutes. Drain and rinse the beans, and add them to the pan to warm through for 4–5 minutes.

Meanwhile, mash the avocado flesh in a bowl and add the lime juice and chopped chilli/chile. Season to taste.

For the dressing, whisk the chipotle paste, oil, vinegar and sugar together and season to taste.

Spread each of the tortillas with some of the avocado spread and pile with some of the bean mixture. Drizzle over some of the dressing, and scatter with a few chopped spring onions/scallions and some coriander/cilantro leaves. Roll up and serve with vegan soured/sour cream.

MOLE-STYLE MUSHROOMS

2 dried ancho chillies/chiles
2 onions, sliced
3 tablespoons olive oil
2 tablespoons ground cumin
1 tablespoon dried oregano
1–2 tablespoons smoked paprika
1 tablespoon fennel seeds
2 x 400-g/14-oz. cans chopped tomatoes
50 g/½ cup ground almonds
1 kg/35 oz. mushrooms, stalks removed (I use a mix of white and chestnut)
200 ml/¾–1 cup chilli/chile soaking water
300 ml/1¼ cups well-flavoured vegetable stock
2 tablespoons caster/granulated sugar
100 g/3½ oz. sultanas or raisins
80 g/3 oz. vegan 70% dark chocolate

SERVES 4

Rich, chilli/chile-charged mole sauces are super-popular in Mexican cuisine – they often include dark chocolate to give them a unique and delicious tang.

Preheat the oven to 190°C (375°F) Gas 5. Put the dried ancho chillies/chiles into a jug/pitcher and cover with water. Leave to soak for about 30 minutes.

Meanwhile, scatter the onions into the base of a deep sheet pan. Pour over the oil and stir in the cumin, oregano, paprika and fennel seeds. Roast for 10–15 minutes, until the onions have started to soften.

Remove the ancho chillies/chiles from the soaking water (reserve the water), cut off the tops (no need to remove the seeds), and blitz them in a food processor with the tomatoes and ground almonds. Pour the mixture into the softened onions, add the mushrooms, the chilli/chile soaking water and stock. Stir in the sugar and sultanas or raisins. Break the chocolate into small pieces and add it to the pan too. Cook for about 45 minutes, until the sauce is thickened. Serve.

MEXICAN VEGETABLE & KIDNEY BEAN BAKE WITH AVOCADO HOLLANDAISE

This is a meat-free chilli/chili that will tempt carnivores, vegetarians and vegans alike. It doesn't pack too much of a punch, making it family-friendly, but chilli/chili-fiends could add some dried chilli/hot red pepper flakes, a slick of chilli oil, or even a scattering of some freshly chopped chilli/chile. The avocado 'hollandaise' lifts the whole dish to another level, so do make sure to serve the two together.

1 onion, chopped
3 celery stalks, chopped
2 garlic cloves, finely chopped
3 sweet potatoes, peeled and diced
2 carrots, diced
2 yellow (bell) peppers, deseeded and
    cut into strips
1 red (bell) pepper, deseeded and
    cut into strips
250 g/9 oz. chestnut mushrooms, sliced
450 g/1 lb. cherry tomatoes
4–5 tablespoons olive oil
2 teaspoons ground cumin
2 teaspoons ground coriander
2 teaspoons chilli/chili powder
2 teaspoons caster/granulated sugar
600 ml/2½ cups passata/strained tomatoes
2 tablespoons good-quality tomato ketchup
400-g/14-oz. can red kidney beans, drained
    and rinsed
2 handfuls of fresh baby spinach leaves
a handful of freshly chopped coriander/
    cilantro
sea salt and freshly ground black pepper

for the avocado hollandaise
1 large, ripe avocado
juice of ½ lemon
50 ml/3½ tablespoons water
2 tablespoons olive oil

SERVES 4

Preheat the oven to 180°C (350°F) Gas 4. Scatter the onion, celery and garlic into a deep sheet pan.

Add the sweet potatoes, carrots, (bell) peppers, mushrooms and cherry tomatoes to the pan. Drizzle in the olive oil, add the spices and sugar, season with salt and freshly ground black pepper and roast for 20–35 minutes, until the vegetables have started to soften and brown. Remove from the oven and stir in the passata/strained tomotoes and ketchup. Cook for a further 30 minutes.

Remove from the oven, stir in the kidney beans, spinach and half of the coriander/cilantro. Return to the oven for about 5 minutes, until the spinach is just about wilted. Scatter over the remaining coriander/cilantro.

In the meantime, make the avocado hollandaise. Peel the avocado and remove the pit. Chop the flesh and pop it into the bowl of a blender (alternatively, use a jug/pitcher and a stick blender). Add the lemon juice, water and olive oil and whiz to a smooth purée. Season to taste, transfer to a small bowl and serve alongside the vegetable and kidney bean bake.

SIDES & SALADS

TWICE-BAKED CHEESY POTATOES

These potatoes are almost a meal in themselves and are delicious alongside a crisp salad and fresh tomatoes. Alternatively, enjoy a half filled potato as your carbohydrate portion in your main meal.

2 large baking potatoes
40 g/⅓ cup grated/shredded Cheddar cheese
60 g/¼ cup soured cream
½ teaspoon sea salt

SERVES 4
AS A SIDE DISH

Preheat the oven to 220°C (425°F) Gas 7.

Pierce the baking potatoes lightly with a fork. Put the potatoes on the middle shelf of the preheated oven and bake for 45 minutes until tender.

Remove the potatoes from the oven and carefully slice in half. Scoop out the insides of the potatoes using a blunt knife or spoon, being careful not to slit the skin. Mash the potato flesh with the grated/shredded cheese until the cheese is all melted, then mash in the soured cream and salt.

Put the potato skins on a sheet pan and fill the skins with the cheesy mash. Bake for a further 15 minutes. Serve immediately.

PERFECT ROAST POTATOES

Who doesn't love a perfectly roasted potato? I'll admit that it took me a while and a consultation with my mother before reaching a method of producing perfectly roasted potatoes that I was happy with. This is the result.

2.5 kg/5½ lb. potatoes, such as Maris Piper, peeled and quartered lengthways
5 tablespoons goose or duck fat (or an non-animal fat if vegetarian/vegan)
sea salt and freshly ground black pepper

SERVES 6
AS A SIDE DISH

Preheat the oven to 200°C (400°F) Gas 6.

Put the potatoes in a large saucepan, cover with water and add a little salt. Bring to the boil, then simmer for 8 minutes. Drain really well, tossing in a colander so all surfaces of the potatoes dry.

On the hob, heat the fat in a sheet pan with sides (not one with a non-stick coating). Toss the potatoes in the fat. Season well with salt and pepper.

Continue cooking on the hob and once all surfaces of the potatoes are starting to brown, put the potatoes in the preheated oven and roast for 40 minutes or until crispy. Serve.

PAN HAGGERTY

This is a traditional stovetop-one-pan-potato-dish that comes from the north of England, and very tasty it is too. Here, I've given it the sheet pan treatment, and I think it's fab. You might want to line the sheet pan with baking parchment or a silicone mat because the crispy bits around the edges do tend to stick.

1 kg/35 oz. floury potatoes, peeled and thinly sliced
3 brown or white onions, thinly sliced
3–4 tablespoons olive oil
250 g/2¾ cups extra mature Cheddar cheese, grated
a small handful of fresh thyme leaves
mixed salad, to serve

SERVES 4

Preheat the oven to 190°C (375°F) Gas 5.

Put the sliced potatoes and onions into a bowl. Pour in the olive oil and add all but a handful of the cheese. Add the thyme leaves and toss everything together so that the onions and the cheese are evenly distributed. Spread the mixture evenly over a greased or lined sheet pan and cover with foil. Bake for about 50 minutes, and then remove the foil and scatter over the remaining cheese. Bake for a further 10 minutes or so, until the cheese is melted and golden.

Serve hot, with a mixed salad.

ROSEMARY & THYME ANNA POTATOES

In my work as a professional private chef, I often serve Anna potatoes – they seem to be universally loved. Of course then, I make sure to painstakingly arrange the potatoes in concentric-slightly-overlapping layers. At home, I just freestyle – as long as they're level in the pan to make sure that they cook evenly, I think a more relaxed presentation is quite nice – but feel free to be more precise if you're cooking them with a special meal in mind.

1 kg/35 oz. floury potatoes, peeled and very thinly sliced
150 g/⅔ cup melted butter
1 tablespoon fresh thyme leaves
2 tablespoons freshly chopped rosemary
sea salt and freshly ground black pepper
a 30 x 17 x 2.5 cm/11¾ x 6¾ x 1 inch brownie pan, lightly greased and lined with baking parchment

SERVES 4-6

Preheat the oven to 200°C (400°F) Gas 6.

Don't wash the potato slices, as the starch in them will help them stick together – simply put them into a large bowl and pour in the melted butter (I melt the butter in the oven, but a microwave will do, if you prefer). Add the herbs and season with salt and freshly ground black pepper, then give everything a really good stir, so that the butter and herbs thoroughly coat the potato slices. Spread the potatoes in the prepared brownie pan, cover with foil and bake for about 50 minutes–1 hour, removing the foil halfway through the cooking time, until the potatoes are soft and golden on the top. Serve immediately.

ROAST BUTTERNUT SQUASH WITH BLACK BELUGA LENTILS, POMEGRANATES & PINE NUTS

2 small butternut squash, halved
  and deseeded
4–5 tablespoons olive oil
a handful of fresh thyme leaves
2 tablespoons freshly chopped rosemary
2 large leeks, trimmed and chopped
300 g/10½ oz. baby plum tomatoes
1 x 400-g/14-oz. can black beluga lentils
sea salt flakes and freshly ground
  black pepper

for the dressing
50 ml/3½ tablespoons olive oil
50 ml/3½ tablespoons pomegranate
  molasses

to serve
50 g/scant ½ cup toasted pine nuts
3–4 tablespoons pomegranate seeds
rocket/arugula leaves

SERVES 4

Roasting the squash in its skin gives the whole vegetable such a fabulous texture and the skin is unbelievably good to eat. Serve with a rocket/arugula salad.

Preheat the oven to 190°C (375°F) Gas 5. Lightly score a diamond pattern into the flesh of the squash using the tip of a sharp knife. Drizzle with a little of the oil, sprinkle with the thyme and rosemary, place on a flat sheet pan and bake for 15 minutes.

Remove the sheet pan from the oven and push the squash over to one side. Scatter the chopped leeks and whole baby plum tomatoes on the other side of the pan and drizzle with the remaining oil. Scatter with salt flakes and freshly ground black pepper and return to the oven for another 20 minutes, until the flesh of the squash is soft and the leeks and tomatoes are lightly charred.

Scoop the leeks and tomatoes into a large bowl. Drain and rinse the lentils, and add them to the bowl. Mix the olive oil and pomegranate molasses together for the dressing and add about half to the lentil mixture. Pile the mixture into the squash hollows and return the sheet pan to the oven. Bake for 5 minutes, until the lentil filling is just heated through.

Remove from the oven, drizzle over the remaining dressing, scatter with pine nuts and pomegranate seeds and add a good grinding of black pepper.

PARSNIPS MOLLY PARKIN

This dish was originally developed by a friend of the Welsh journalist and top parsnip hater Molly Parkin, in order to convince her they were a vegetable more than worthy of her affection. He fried them in a pan and layered them in a dish with sliced tomatoes, cheese and cream and she did, in fact, change her mind.

750 g/26 oz. parsnips
4 tablespoons olive oil
1 leek
400 g/14 oz. cherry tomatoes, halved
400 ml/1¾ cups double/heavy cream
200 g/2¼ cups strong cheese, such
  as Mature Cheddar or Gruyère, grated
50 g/1 cup panko crumbs
sea salt flakes and freshly ground
  black pepper
green salad, to serve

SERVES 4

Preheat the oven to 190°C (375°F) Gas 5.

Peel the parsnips and cut them into slices. Arrange them over a deep sheet pan and drizzle with the olive oil. Roast for about 20 minutes, until they are light golden and just starting to soften. Wash and trim the leek and cut it into slices. Add it to the sheet pan and roast for a further 10 minutes.

Carefully mix the cherry tomatoes into the roasted vegetables. Mix the cream and all but a small handful of the cheese together. Season with salt flakes and freshly ground black pepper. Pour the mixture over the vegetables, and then scatter the remaining cheese and the panko crumbs over the top. Bake for a further 10–15 minutes, until everything is bubbling hot and the crumbs are golden. Serve with a green salad.

FONDANT TOMATOES WITH BASIL & BURRATA

Warm, sweet roasted baby plum tomatoes and fridge-cold creamy burrata make a combination that is out-of-this-world irresistible. Be generous with the extra virgin olive oil, as it will help create the most incredible juices, which marry together with those from the tomatoes and create something magical when they meet with the dreamy burrata.

500 g/18 oz. baby plum tomatoes, halved
300 g/10½ oz. baby plum tomatoes
   on the vine
4–5 tablespoons olive oil
2 teaspoons caster/granulated sugar
2 teaspoons fresh thyme leaves
400 g/14 oz. (drained weight) burrata
sea salt and freshly ground black pepper
fresh basil leaves, to garnish

SERVES 4

Preheat the oven to 150°C (300°F) Gas 2.

Lay the baby plum tomatoes, cut side up, on a large, flat sheet pan. Cut the baby tomatoes on the vine into little clusters of two or three, and arrange them on the sheet pan as well. Drizzle with the oil, sprinkle with sugar and season with salt and freshly ground black pepper. Scatter over the thyme leaves. Cook for about 30 minutes or so – until the tomatoes are meltingly soft and sticky.

Remove from the oven and leave to cool slightly. Gently tear the burrata into pieces and arrange it over the tomatoes. Scatter with fresh basil leaves and serve warm with crusty bread for dipping into the juices.

BABY PLUM TOMATO CLAFOUTIS

You may well have come across a cherry clafoutis – the classic French dessert that's not quite a custard, nor an omelette, nor a gratin, but is nevertheless very well loved. This is my savoury version, and it makes a first-rate dish for a light lunch. It's great for a picnic basket too.

8 eggs
120 g/1⅓ cups extra mature Cheddar
   cheese, grated
95 g/⅔ cup plain/all-purpose flour
300 ml/10½ fl. oz. double/heavy cream
300 g/10½ oz. baby plum tomatoes
   (or use cherry tomatoes)
30 g/scant ½ cup Parmesan cheese
sea salt and freshly ground black pepper
fresh basil leaves, to garnish
a 30 x 17 x 2.5 cm/11¾ x 6¾ x 1 inch
   brownie pan, lightly greased and lined
   with baking parchment

SERVES 4–6

Preheat the oven to 190°C (375°F) Gas 5.

Beat the eggs well, and then stir in the grated cheese. Slowly add in the flour, whisking until it has been fully incorporated. Stir in the cream. Season the mixture with salt and freshly ground black pepper. Pour the mixture into the prepared pan and scatter the tomatoes evenly over. Bake for about 20–25 minutes, until the clafoutis has set.

Make shavings from the Parmesan using a potato peeler and sprinkle them across the top of the clafoutis. Garnish with fresh basil leaves, cut into squares and serve.

ROASTED MEDITERRANEAN VEGETABLES WITH BALSAMIC DRESSING

When I say '1 fairly large courgette/zucchini' here, I don't mean the sort that is on the verge of classification as a small marrow – huge courgettes/zucchinis might look fairly impressive on the outside, but the flesh can become quite lacking in flavour, as the water content rises and the seeds become bigger – often giving the vegetable a slightly bitter taste. Make sure to roast until the vegetables are looking a little charred at the edges here and there – it will take the best part of an hour, but will reward with bags of flavour.

2 red onions, cut into wedges
1 fairly large courgette/zucchini, sliced
1 medium aubergine/eggplant, cut into
   bite-sized chunks
1 red (bell) pepper, deseeded and cut
   into strips
1 yellow (bell) pepper, deseeded and cut
   into strips
1 orange (bell) pepper, deseeded and cut
   into strips
400 g/14 oz. cherry tomatoes
5 tablespoons olive oil
a good scattering of fresh thyme leaves
3 tablespoons balsamic vinegar
sea salt flakes and freshly ground
   black pepper
fresh basil leaves, to garnish

SERVES 4

Preheat the oven to 190°C (375°F) Gas 5.

Scatter the onion wedges over a sheet pan. Scatter the courgette/zucchini, aubergine/eggplant and (bell) peppers over the pan. Leave the tomatoes whole and scatter the tomatoes over. Drizzle everything with the oil, season with salt flakes, freshly ground black pepper and lots of fresh thyme leaves. Cook for 50 minutes–1 hour, turning everything halfway through the cooking time, until the vegetables are shiny and soft, and lightly charred at the edges.

Drizzle over the balsamic vinegar, garnish with fresh basil leaves and serve warm or at room temperature.

CHARRED TURNIP, RADISH & RED ONION SALAD WITH ROASTED GARLIC (NO EGG) MAYONNAISE

Turnips probably don't have the biggest fan club, but when roasted, the transformation is spectacular.

400 g/14 oz. radishes
400 g/14 oz. small turnips, cut into quarters
4 red onions, cut into wedges
1 whole bulb fresh garlic
4 tablespoons olive oil
1 teaspoon caster/granulated sugar
1 tablespoon fresh thyme leaves
150 g/5½ oz. red chicory/endive
dill fronds, to garnish

for the (no egg) mayonnaise
2 tablespoons chickpea water (aquafaba)
1 scant tablespoon Dijon mustard
2 tablespoons cider vinegar
150 ml/⅔ cup sunflower oil
sea salt

SERVES 4

Preheat the oven to 200°C (400°F) Gas 6.

Scatter the radishes, turnips and red onions over a large sheet pan. Cut the whole garlic bulb in half horizontally and lay it in the corner of the sheet pan, cut sides up. Drizzle everything with the olive oil. Sprinkle the radishes, turnips and onions with the sugar, but avoid the garlic. Scatter over the thyme leaves. Bake for 35 minutes, until the vegetables are soft and golden and slightly charred. Remove from the oven, leave to cool slightly, and transfer to a pretty platter. Arrange the red chicory/endive leaves here and there and garnish with dill fronds.

For the (no egg) mayonnaise, put the chickpea water, mustard and cider vinegar into a jug and add a pinch of salt. Blitz with a stick blender until mixed. Slowly pour in the sunflower oil, until the mixture has emulsified and thickened. Squeeze the roasted garlic out of the crispy little compartments of skin into the mixture and blitz again until well mixed. Serve with the charred turnip and radish salad.

TAMARIND & ROSEMARY SWEET POTATOES WITH SHALLOTS & TOASTED HAZELNUTS

This top-notch combo makes a really good side dish, but could be served as a main alongside a green salad or some lightly cooked greens. Although its actually vegan-friendly, you could happily feed it to the most staunch carnivore and I'm certain they wouldn't miss the meat for a minute.

1 kg/35 oz. sweet potatoes, peeled and
    chopped into chunks
300 g/10½ oz. shallots
40 g/1½ oz. tamarind paste
40 g/1½ oz. brown rice syrup
40 ml/scant 3 tablespoons olive oil
2 tablespoons finely chopped rosemary
100 g/3½ oz. whole hazelnuts, lightly crushed

SERVES 4

Preheat the oven to 190°C (375°F) Gas 5.

Put the sweet potatoes into a large bowl. Peel the shallots and add to the bowl. Mix the tamarind paste with the brown rice syrup, olive oil and rosemary. Add to the bowl and toss everything together. Arrange over a large sheet pan. Roast for 15 minutes.

Scatter over the hazelnuts and cook for a further 15 minutes, until the vegetables are soft and golden. Serve straight away.

COURGETTE & SUN-DRIED TOMATO FRITTERS WITH SUMAC KEFALOTYRI

450 g/1 lb. courgettes/zucchinis, topped
  and tailed
scant 1 teaspoon fine sea salt
80 g/3 oz. sun-dried tomatoes,
  roughly chopped
a generous bunch of spring onions/scallions,
  chopped
2 tablespoons fine polenta/cornmeal
  or semolina
scant 1 teaspoon baking powder
1 egg, beaten
4–5 tablespoons olive oil
150 g/5½ oz. Kefalotyri cheese, cut into
  small cubes
1 teaspoon ground sumac
freshly ground black pepper
fresh mint leaves and mixed salad, to serve

SERVES 4
(MAKES 8 FRITTERS)

Kefalotyri is a hard cheese from Greece and Cyprus, not dissimilar to halloumi. When oven-baked, it takes on a gorgeous golden colour and has a slightly stringy melting texture and an agreeably salty flavour.

Preheat the oven to 200°C (400°F) Gas 6. Coarsely grate the courgettes/zucchini and put them into a large sieve/strainer. Sprinkle over the salt and leave to stand for about 10 minutes. Squeeze the courgettes/zucchinis to remove as much water as possible, and then transfer them to a large bowl. Add the sun-dried tomato pieces, spring onions/scallions, polenta/cornmeal and baking powder and then stir in the egg until everything is evenly mixed. Season with a little freshly ground black pepper (you shouldn't need to add any additional salt).

Brush a large sheet pan with a little of the oil and drop tablespoonfuls of the mixture over the pan. Bake for 15 minutes. Brush the tops of the fritters with a little of the oil and turn them over. Return to the oven for 5 minutes. In the meantime, toss the cheese cubes with the remaining oil and the sumac, and then arrange them over the fritters. Bake for a further 15 minutes, until the cheese is golden and melted. Garnish with mint leaves and serve with a mixed salad.

WARM HALLOUMI, FIG & PISTACHIO SALAD

400 g/14 oz. halloumi cheese, cut into
  bite-sized pieces
4 tablespoons olive oil
1–2 teaspoons ras el hanout spice mix
8–10 firm, but ripe figs
1–2 tablespoons runny honey
2 handfuls of pistachios, crushed
1 tablespoon balsamic vinegar
fresh mint leaves, to garnish

SERVES 4

I have never, ever once been able to resist picking at the cheese when I open the oven door and it's there in front of me looking all golden and gorgeous and flecked with spices. Of course, when it's served with warm, sweet figs, drizzled with honey and scattered with pistachios and mint, its moreish appeal climbs up several notches more, so I really should have more patience, I suppose.

Preheat the oven to 190°C (375°F) Gas 5. Arrange the halloumi pieces in a roasting pan. Drizzle over half of the oil and add the ras el hanout. Carefully toss the cheese and spice mix together so that the cheese is evenly coated. Roast for 10 minutes, until the halloumi is soft and golden. Cut the figs into quarters and arrange them over the pan. Drizzle with the honey and return to the oven for 5–6 minutes, until the figs are warm and soft, but still holding their shape. Scatter over the crushed pistachios. Mix the balsamic vinegar with the remaining olive oil and drizzle it over everything. Garnish with mint leaves and serve warm.

CAULIFLOWER, SULTANA & MANGO SALAD WITH LENTILS & TURMERIC, GINGER & MAPLE DRESSING

The fresh turmeric dressing takes this dish to another level. Neon-orange turmeric root has a more zippy flavour than dried turmeric. Its increasing popularity means that it is now fairly readily available.

1 large cauliflower (500 g/18 oz. trimmed weight in florets)
6 tablespoons olive oil
1 tablespoon ground coriander
1 tablespoon ground cumin
1 tablespoon fennel seeds
1 teaspoon dried chilli/red pepper flakes
1 tablespoon demerara sugar
2 red (bell) peppers, deseeded and cut into strips
3 red onions, cut into wedges
200 g/7 oz. cherry tomatoes, halved
1 x 400-g/14-oz. can black beluga lentils, drained and rinsed
2–3 tablespoons sultanas/golden raisins
1 small, ripe mango, peeled, pitted and diced
a bunch of fresh coriander/cilantro, roughly chopped
sea salt and freshly ground black pepper

for the dressing
25 g/1 oz. fresh turmeric, peeled and finely grated
2 cm/¾ inch knob of fresh ginger, peeled and grated
2 garlic cloves, finely grated
2 tablespoons tahini paste
zest and juice of 1 lime
50 ml/3½ tablespoons water
4 tablespoons olive oil
1 teaspoon caster/granulated sugar
1–2 tablespoons maple syrup

SERVES 4

Preheat the oven to 190°C (375°F) Gas 5. Break the cauliflower into florets. Pour the oil into a large bowl, and add the coriander, cumin, fennel seeds, chilli/red pepper flakes and sugar. Give everything a good stir, season with salt and pepper, and toss the cauliflower florets into the mixture to coat. Spread them over a large sheet pan. Scatter the red (bell) peppers, onion wedges and cherry tomatoes over the sheet pan and mix. Roast for 20–25 minutes (give everything a stir halfway through the cooking time), until the cauliflower is cooked but still has some bite.

Stir the lentils gently into the roasted vegetables. Return the sheet pan to the oven for 5 minutes, until the lentils are just heated through. Remove the pan from the oven and scatter over the sultanas/raisins. Scatter the mango over the salad and garnish with the coriander/cilantro. For the dressing, put the grated turmeric and ginger into a bowl. Add all the remaining ingredients and whisk together until smooth. Season to taste, drizzle over the salad and serve.

SPICED TOMATOES WITH PANEER & PEAS

450 g/1 lb. paneer, cut into 1-cm/½-in. dice
3 tablespoons olive oil
2 teaspoons ground cumin
2 teaspoons ground coriander
1 teaspoon ground turmeric

for the sauce
2 onions, sliced
4 large ripe tomatoes, roughly chopped
500 g/18 oz. passata/strained tomatoes
5-cm/2-inch piece of root of ginger, chopped
2 garlic cloves, finely chopped
50 g/½ cup ground almonds
300 g/scant 2½ cups frozen peas
a handful of chopped coriander/cilantro
extra chopped coriander/cilantro, mango chutney and naan bread, to serve

SERVES 4

Paneer is really useful to keep in the fridge for vegetarians. When you stir it into pungent spice mixes and lip-smacking sauces, it happily seems to slurp up the flavours amazingly well. I love this with mango chutney and peshwari naan.

Preheat the oven to 190°C (375°F) Gas 5. Put the paneer into a large bowl. Add the oil, cumin, coriander and turmeric and give everything a good stir to coat the paneer. Transfer to a deep sheet pan. Roast for 10 minutes. Meanwhile, for the sauce, add the onions to the bowl you were using for the paneer. Add the tomatoes and pour in the passata/strained tomatoes. Stir the ginger into the tomato mix together with the garlic. Add the ground almonds and mix.

Remove the paneer from the oven and pour over the tomato mix. Return to the oven for 20 minutes. Stir in the peas and chopped coriander/cilantro and return to the oven for 5 minutes more. Serve with extra chopped coriander/cilantro, mango chutney and naan bread for scooping.

SALT-BAKED HERITAGE BEETROOT & MANGO LETTUCE CUPS WITH NERIGOMA DRESSING

800 g/4 cups coarse sea salt
3 egg whites
4 candy-striped and yellow beetroots/beets
50 ml/3½ tablespoons olive oil
juice of 2 limes
1 teaspoon caster/granulated sugar
1 small red onion, sliced
1 large, ripe but firm tomato,
   roughly chopped
1 medium, ripe mango, peeled, pitted
   and diced
a small of handful of freshly chopped
   coriander/cilantro
sea salt and freshly ground black pepper
iceberg or Little Gem lettuce cups
fresh mint leaves, to garnish

for the nerigoma dressing
4 tablespoons nerigoma
zest and juice of 1 lime
1 garlic clove, finely grated
3–4 tablespoons water

SERVES 4

Salt-baking seems to intensify the sweetness of beetroot/beet. If you can manage to find different coloured beetroots/beets, it makes this a very beautiful dish. Served in lettuce cups, it makes a very special dinner party starter.

Preheat the oven to 190°C (375°F) Gas 5. Put the salt into a large bowl and mix in the egg whites. Spread about a third of the mixture in a thin layer on a lined sheet pan. Place the beetroots/beets close together, and then pat the remaining salt mixture over the beetroots/beets to cover them. Bake for about 1 hour, until the beetroots/beets seem to be soft when tested with the point of a knife.

Meanwhile, mix the olive oil, lime juice and sugar in a large bowl. Season.

When the beetroots/beets are cooked, give the salt crust a good thwack with a rolling pin, and remove them. Once the beetroots/beets are cool enough, gently peel away the skin and cut them into dice. Drop them into the lime dressing whilst they are still warm, and leave to cool completely. Add the onion, tomato and mango to the dressing and stir in the chopped coriander/cilantro.

Whisk all the ingredients for the nerigoma dressing together. Carefully peel away layers of the lettuce to make cups and fill them with the beetroot/beet mixture. Garnish with mint leaves, and serve with the nerigoma dressing.

BAKED SWEET POTATOES WITH MISO BUTTER, CHIVES & BLACK SESAME SEEDS

4 medium sweet potatoes
3 tablespoons olive oil
1–2 tablespoons fresh thyme leaves

for the miso butter
150 g/1¼ sticks butter, softened
20 g/¾ oz. white miso paste
a bunch of chives, chopped
1 tablespoon black sesame seeds
rocket/arugula salad, to serve

SERVES 4

Miso adds the most glorious, rich, umami flavour to anything it touches. When you beat a small amount into creamy butter and let it melt over hot sweet potatoes you'll find your taste buds dancing the sprightliest of tangos.

Preheat the oven to 190°C (375°F) Gas 5. Wash the sweet potatoes and cut them in half from tip to tip. Lay them on a sheet pan, cut side up, score the flesh lightly with a diamond pattern, and drizzle them with oil. Scatter over the thyme leaves. Transfer to the oven and roast for about 35–40 minutes, until very soft.

Beat the butter and miso paste together, until evenly combined. Stir in half of the chopped chives. Remove the sweet potatoes from the oven and mash the centres of each roughly, using a fork. Spoon over some miso butter, and sprinkle over the black sesame seeds and remaining chives. Serve hot with a salad.

CRISPY BENGALI 5 SPICE POTATOES WITH SPRING ONIONS & CHILLI & CORIANDER RAITA

for the panch phoran spice mix
10 g/⅓ oz. nigella (black onion) seeds
10 g/⅓ oz. cumin seeds
10 g/⅓ oz. black mustard seeds
10 g/⅓ oz. fenugreek seeds
10 g/⅓ oz. fennel seeds

500 g/18 oz. floury potatoes
50 g/1¾ oz. panch phoran spice mix
4–5 tablespoons olive oil
a large bunch of spring onions/
  scallions, sliced
1–2 red chillies/chiles, deseeded and sliced
sea salt flakes and freshly ground black pepper

for the raita
200 g/scant 1 cup full fat plain/
  natural yogurt
2 garlic cloves, grated
a handful of freshly chopped coriander/cilantro

SERVES 4

Panch phoran is an amazing aromatic mix of five whole spices that originally hails from Bengal and Eastern India. It adds the wow factor to all manner of dishes – from hearty curries to simple steamed veg. You can buy it as a ready-made mix, but it's such a doddle to make, you may just as well rustle up your own.

Preheat the oven to 190°C (375°F) Gas 5. Combine all the whole seeds together for the spice mix.

Peel the potatoes, and cut them into small dice – about 15 mm/⅝ inch square. Put them into a bowl and add the panch phoran spice mix. Add the oil, and then toss everything together until the potatoes are evenly coated in the spices. Arrange them evenly over a large, flat sheet pan and roast for about 50 minutes or so – until they are golden and crisp. Remove from the oven and season with salt flakes. Scatter the spring onions/scallions and chillies/chiles over the potatoes.

Meanwhile, put the yogurt into a bowl and stir in the grated garlic and chopped coriander/cilantro. Season with a few salt flakes and a little freshly ground black pepper. Serve alongside the Bengali 5 spice potatoes.

CRISPY RICE WITH SOY & GINGER TEMPEH

At first glance, soy-rice-speckled tempeh seems neither attractive nor inspiring – but its saving grace is that it does absorb strong flavours and marinades very well. It responds well to baking too, so this is one of those dishes that die hard meat-eaters are really very pleasantly surprised by.

200 g/7 oz. tempeh
5 tablespoons dark soy sauce
1 tablespoon sesame oil
1 teaspoon caster/granulated sugar
30 g/1 oz. fresh ginger, finely grated
2 garlic cloves, finely grated
200 g/generous 1 cup basmati rice
3 tablespoons olive oil
a bunch of spring onions/scallions, chopped
a bunch of freshly chopped coriander/cilantro
1 tablespoon white sesame seeds, to garnish

SERVES 4

Preheat the oven to 190°C (375°F) Gas 5. Cut the tempeh into slices. Mix the soy sauce, sesame oil and sugar together in a large bowl. Stir in the grated ginger and garlic. Toss the tempeh slices in the mixture and leave to marinate.

Rinse the rice under running water, until the water runs clear. Scatter it over the base of a lined, deep sheet pan. Pour in 800 ml/scant 3½ cups water and bake for about 30 minutes, until the water has been absorbed and the rice is cooked. Remove the pan from the oven and drizzle over the olive oil. Remove the tempeh from the marinade and lay it in a row down the centre of the rice. Return to the oven and bake for about 10 minutes, until the tempeh is hot and the rice is crisp. Scatter over the spring onions/scallions, coriander/cilantro and sesame seeds, and serve.

JERK VEGGIE SKEWERS WITH CELERIAC, SULTANA & CAPER SALAD

1 red, 1 yellow and 1 orange (bell) pepper, deseeded and cut into strips
2 red onions, cut into wedges
2 medium courgettes/zucchinis, thickly sliced
200 g/7 oz. baby button mushrooms
200 g/7 oz. baby plum or cherry tomatoes
6 tablespoons olive oil
3 tablespoons jerk spice mix
2 teaspoons light muscovado sugar

for the salad
1 small celeriac/celery root
2 crisp eating apples
50 g/⅓ cup sultanas/golden raisins
1 tablespoon capers, drained
a small bunch of freshly chopped parsley
(No Egg) Mayonnaise (page 144), to serve

8 long, wooden skewers

SERVES 4

I've teamed the zippy skewers up with a dreamy salad of crisp celeriac/celery root and apple, peppered with salty capers and sweet plump sultanas/golden raisins. Simplicity at its delicious best.

Preheat the oven to 200°C (400°F) Gas 6. Push the prepared vegetables, mushrooms and tomatoes onto the skewers, alternating them as you go. Lay them on a large, flat sheet pan.

Mix the oil, jerk spice mix and sugar together in a bowl and brush this over the vegetables. Transfer the pan to the oven and roast for 15–20 minutes, until the vegetables are soft, but retaining a little bite.

To make the salad, peel the celeriac/celery root, cut it into slices and then into fine julienne. Transfer to a large bowl. Core the apples, cut them into similar sized strips and add them into your bowl, together with the sultanas/raisins and capers.

Add the (No Egg) Mayonnaise (page 144) to the celeriac/celery root and apple salad and stir in the chopped parsley. Serve alongside the veggie skewers.

TRINIDADIAN VEGETABLE PELAU

1 onion, chopped
2 large carrots, diced
2 celery stalks, diced
1 yellow (bell) pepper, deseeded and diced
1 red (bell) pepper, deseeded and diced
20 g/1 tablespoon plus 1 teaspoon light brown muscovado sugar
3 tablespoons olive oil
2 garlic cloves, grated
50 g/1¾ oz. ginger root, peeled and grated
300 g/1¾ cups wholegrain basmati rice
2 x 400-g/14-oz. cans coconut milk
1 x 400-g/14-oz. can black-eyed beans
1 teaspoon fresh thyme leaves
1 red chilli/chile, deseeded and chopped
a bunch of spring onions/scallions, chopped
a bunch of coriander/cilantro, chopped
sea salt and freshly ground black pepper

SERVES 4

Based on the traditional Trinidadian rice dish, pelau, this dish has an irresistible hint of sweetness that contrasts beautifully with the kick of ginger and chilli/chile.

Preheat the oven to 190°C (375°F) Gas 5. Scatter the chopped onion over the base of a deep sheet pan. Add the carrots, celery and (bell) peppers to the pan. Sprinkle over the muscovado sugar and stir in the olive oil. Transfer the pan to the oven and cook for 15 minutes.

Remove the pan from the oven and add the garlic and ginger. Put the rice into a sieve, rinse it until the water runs clear and add it to the pan. Stir in the coconut milk and 400 ml/scant 1¾ cups water. Drain and rinse the beans and add them to the pelau with the thyme leaves and chopped chilli/chile. Return the sheet pan to the oven and cook for a further 40 minutes or so, until the rice is cooked and all the liquid is absorbed.

Season to taste, stir in the spring onions/scallions and coriander/cilantro, and serve with extra chopped chilli/chile, if desired.

OVEN-ROASTED CHILLI JAM

Sticky, spicy, and bursting with vibrant colour and flavour, this chilli/chile jam makes a great accompaniment to a whole host of different dishes. If I have the oven on and some tomatoes that need using, there's every chance I'll end up putting on a batch of this lovely condiment because somehow, my fridge always feels more complete when I know I have some in there, even though it seems to disappear as quickly as I make it.

1 kg/35 oz. fresh tomatoes
5–6 red chillies/chiles, stalks removed
100 ml/⅓ cup plus 1 tablespoon white wine vinegar
6-cm/2½-inch piece of root ginger
300 g/1½ cups caster/granulated sugar
3 tablespoons olive oil

SERVES 6-8

Preheat the oven to 190°C (375°F) Gas 5. Put the tomatoes and chillies/chiles into a food processor and blitz until really finely chopped. Pour them into the bottom of a large, deep sheet pan. Stir in the white wine vinegar.

Peel the ginger and chop it very finely. Stir it with the sugar into the tomato mixture and transfer the sheet pan to the oven. Cook for about 1 hour, stirring occasionally, until the tomato mixture is sticky and jam-like.

Add the olive oil, and give the mixture a final stir. Pour into a sterilized airtight jar, seal and cool, then store in the fridge for up to a couple of weeks.

ROASTED RED PEPPER, CHILLI & ALMOND DIP WITH TORTILLA CRISPS

Roasted (bell) pepper yumminess again – this time whizzed into a zippy almond dip and served alongside crunchy tortilla crisps/chips. Piri-piri seasoning is nice on the tortilla crisps/chips too.

2 red (bell) peppers, deseeded and cut into strips
200 g/7 oz. cherry tomatoes
3 tablespoons olive oil
50 g/½ cup ground almonds
2 garlic cloves, chopped
1 teaspoon dried chilli/red pepper flakes
sea salt flakes

for the tortilla crisps/chips
4 flour tortillas
2–3 tablespoons olive oil
1 teaspoon paprika

SERVES 4

Preheat the oven to 190°C (375°F) Gas 5. Scatter the (bell) peppers over a large, flat sheet pan lined with baking parchment along with the cherry tomatoes. Drizzle with the oil, add a scattering of salt flakes and roast for about 20 minutes or so, until the (bell) peppers are cooked and beginning to char, and the tomatoes are soft. Transfer everything to a food processor (you could use a bowl and a stick blender if preferred), making sure to add all the lovely tomatoey juices. Add the ground almonds, chopped garlic and chilli/red pepper flakes and blitz until you have a fairly smooth dip.

Meanwhile, for the tortilla crisps/chips, remove and discard the baking parchment from the sheet pan. Cut the flour tortillas into bite-sized triangular-ish pieces (I always end up with a few wacky shapes too). Put them into a bowl and toss with the olive oil, paprika and some salt flakes. Spread them over the sheet pan and pop them into the oven for about 4–5 minutes, until they are golden and crisp. Transfer the dip and the crisps/chips to separate bowls and enjoy!

SWEET THINGS

GRAIN-FREE GRANOLA

Granola gets a bad name for being full of sugar. This granola uses natural sugars and even forgoes the grains to make it more filling. This means that you need less of it and you can layer it with yogurt for a delicious and rather visually impressive dessert, especially if served in glasses or glass pots.

50 g/5 tablespoons coconut oil, melted
65 g/¼ cup maple syrup
100 g/2 cups dried coconut chips or flakes
100 g/1 cup chopped nuts and/or seeds
½ teaspoon ground cinnamon
a handful of dried fruit

SERVES 3

Preheat the oven to 190°C (375°F) Gas 5.

Mix the melted coconut oil and maple syrup together in a small bowl.

Put the coconut chips or flakes, nuts/seeds, cinnamon and dried fruit in a large bowl and mix together. Pour the coconut oil/maple syrup mixture over the dry ingredients and mix well.

Spread the granola out over a sheet pan lined with baking parchment. Bake in the preheated oven for 15–20 minutes until starting to brown, stirring twice during cooking time. Keep a close eye on it, as it will burn easily. Remove from the oven and leave to cool before serving.

ROASTED PINEAPPLE

Succulent and sweet roasted pineapple really goes down a storm. It's ideal served straight from the oven, and after a meal it works well digestively. A little known fact is that pineapple contains bromelain, which is a digestive enzyme.

1 medium pineapple, peeled, cored and
    chopped into 1-cm/½-in. cubes
1 tablespoon coconut sugar
1 tablespoon coconut oil, melted
½ teaspoon ground cinnamon

SERVES 4

Preheat the oven to 220°C (425°F) Gas 7.

Put all the ingredients on a sheet pan with sides and mix together.

Bake in the preheated oven for 15 minutes until caramelized and soft.

Serving Suggestion: Serve hot with whipped cream, crème fraîche or coconut cream.

BANANA BUTTER FLAPJACKS

A flapjack is a tray-baked bar or square made from oats, butter and sugar. This flapjack, however, uses the natural sugars of bananas and honey to sweeten and moisten the bar in place of refined sugar. This is a substantial dessert and one square should suffice, but then you never know.

300 g/10½ oz. ripe peeled bananas, mashed
65 g/4 tablespoons melted butter
40 g/1½ oz. runny honey
1 teaspoon ground cinnamon
225 g/1½ cups rolled oats

20 x 20-cm/8 x 8-in. sheet pan with
    sides, greased

SERVES 9

Preheat the oven to 200°C (400°F) Gas 6.

Mix all of the ingredients together in a large bowl.

Press the mixture evenly over the base of the prepared sheet pan.

Bake in the preheated oven for 20 minutes until golden brown. Remove from the oven and score nine portions.

Once cooled in the pan, cut into nine portions, remove and serve.

BAKED CHOCOLATE BANANAS

This dessert may be reminiscent of childhood campfires, and if that's what it recalls for you then I'm glad because those life moments are special and dear. It's a winning combination this one. Bananas and chocolate were made for each other.

4 bananas, peeled
1 small packet dark chocolate buttons
    (you need about 5 buttons for
    each banana)
½ teaspoon ground cinnamon

SERVES 4

Preheat the oven to 200°C (400°F) Gas 6.

Lay each banana on its side on an individual piece of foil. Slice along the curve of the banana along the top, but only to halfway through the banana.

Put chocolate buttons all the way along the slit. Sprinkle ⅛ teaspoon of the cinnamon over the banana. Wrap the banana in the foil parcel. Place the banana parcels on a sheet pan.

Bake in the preheated oven for 15–20 minutes until the banana is soft and the chocolate melted.

ORANGE-BAKED RHUBARB

Rhubarb has a finite season so make the most of it whilst it is around. Rhubarb and orange are delightful together and make for a fine dessert. This dessert works exceedingly well with something creamy alongside, such as coconut milk yogurt, coconut cream or cream.

400 g/14 oz. rhubarb, rinsed and cut into
   5-cm/2-in. pieces
freshly squeezed zest and juice of 1 orange
1½ tablespoons honey

SERVES 4

Preheat the oven to 180°C (350°F) Gas 4.

Put the rhubarb on a sheet pan with sides. Squeeze over the orange juice and add the zest, then drizzle over the honey and stir everything together.

Bake in the preheated oven for 30 minutes until the rhubarb is soft. Stir once or twice during baking time.

Serving Suggestion: Serve with natural yogurt, coconut cream or cream.

APPLE & BLACKBERRY ALMOND CRUMBLE

Almonds in many forms make a fantastic, more easily digested alternative to grain-based flours for many. They also provide great flavour and texture to dishes such as this delightful crumble.

150 g/1 cup fresh blackberries
1 eating apple, cored, cut into wedges,
   then very thinly sliced
⅛ teaspoon stevia powder
¼ teaspoon ground cinnamon
65 g/½ cup ground almonds
35 g/½ cup flaked/slivered almonds
45 g/3 tablespoons ghee or coconut oil

450-g/1-lb. loaf pan or small baking dish

SERVES 2

Preheat the oven to 200°C (400°F) Gas 6.

Put the blackberries and apple slices in the base of the loaf pan.

In a medium bowl, mix together the stevia, cinnamon, ground and flaked almonds and ghee or coconut oil using a spoon or your fingertips. Tip the crumble mixture over the fruit in an even layer.

Bake in the preheated oven for 25 minutes. Serve.

Serving Suggestion: Serve with coconut cream or cream.

STICKY GINGER CAKE

This is a deliciously moist cake that takes me back to my childhood. According to my own children, this cake is 'the taste of Christmas'.

8 ready-to-eat dried dates
20 ready-to-eat dried prunes
75 g/¼ cup molasses or black treacle
100 g/⅓ cup maple syrup
185 g/¾ cup natural yogurt or use coconut
  yogurt for a dairy-free version
250 ml/1 cup milk (use coconut milk for
  a dairy-free version)
3½ tablespoons olive oil, plus a little extra
  for greasing
2 eggs, beaten
350 g/2½ cups spelt flour
  (or for a gluten-free version use 170 g/1¼
  cups buckwheat flour, 100 g/¾ cup brown
  rice flour, 50 g/⅓ cup tapioca starch,
  40 g/1½ oz. ground flaxseeds/linseeds)
2½ teaspoons ground ginger
2 teaspoons ground cinnamon
1 teaspoon bicarbonate of soda/baking soda*
1 teaspoon baking powder*
*use gluten-free versions if looking to make
  a gluten-free cake

27 x 20-cm/10¾ x 8-in. brownie pan, greased
  and lined with baking parchment

SERVES 15

Preheat the oven to 180°C (350°F) Gas 4.

Put the dates and prunes into a food processor and process to a paste. Add the molasses or treacle, maple syrup, yogurt, milk, olive oil and eggs and process again.

In a separate bowl, combine all the dry ingredients.

Mix the dry ingredients in with the wet ingredients to combine. Pour into the prepared brownie pan.

Bake in the preheated oven for 30 minutes or until a cocktail stick/toothpick inserted into the middle comes out clean.

Remove from the oven and leave to cool a little before slicing into 15 squares before serving. Any leftover portions can be stored in an airtight container for a couple of days in a cool dry place.

WHITE CHOCOLATE, ALMOND & RASPBERRY RIPPLE BROWNIES

These white chocolate brownies seem to spread supreme joy to all who try them, although I feel they're slightly responsible for the spreading of my hips too, as I am unable to stop at eating just one. I'm also very guilty of trimming off the crusts and eating those too – although I do believe that crusts don't count, especially if you eat them standing up.

200 g/1¾ sticks butter, melted
150 g/5½ oz. white chocolate, melted
400 g/2 cups caster/superfine sugar
4 eggs, beaten
100 g/¾ cup plain/all-purpose flour
200 g/2 cups ground almonds
½ teaspoon baking powder
200 g/7 oz. raspberries
1 tablespoon caster/superfine sugar
50 g/1¾ oz. white chocolate, melted,
   to decorate

a 30 x 17 x 2.5 cm/11¾ x 6¾ x 1 inch
   brownie pan, lightly greased and lined
   with baking parchment

MAKES 15

Preheat the oven to 170°C (325°F) Gas 3.

Pour the melted butter and white chocolate into a large bowl and stir in the 400 g/2 cups of sugar. Beat in the eggs. Add the flour, ground almonds and baking powder and beat together until everything is evenly incorporated. Pour the mixture into the prepared brownie pan.

Push the raspberries through a fine sieve/strainer into a bowl, and stir the 1 tablespoon sugar into the purée. Spoon the purée over the top of the brownie mix in generous swirls. Bake for about 45 minutes–1 hour, until golden and firm when gently prodded in the centre with your index finger.

Drizzle over the extra melted white chocolate to decorate, and leave to cool in the pan. Trim the edges and eat them (standing up), cut the brownies into squares and serve.

VEGAN BROWNIES

I won't lie to you – it did take me a few attempts to reach a level of squidginess that I was really happy with here – but I got there in the end! These lovely, dark, dense brownies are sure to delight chocolate-loving vegans, but I think they will also surprise conventional brownie fans too. They're fab served warm, with a good dairy-free ice cream – but are equally nice served cold with a cuppa.

200 g/7 oz. dark/bittersweet
   chocolate, melted
250 ml /1 cup plus 1 tablespoon
   just-boiled water
100 ml/⅓ cup plus 1 tablespoon
   sunflower oil
375 g/2 cups minus 2
   tablespoons light brown
   muscovado sugar
1 teaspoon cider vinegar

2 teaspoon vanilla bean paste
175 g/1⅓ cups plain/
   all-purpose flour
½ teaspoon baking powder

a 30 x 17 x 2.5 cm/
   11¾ x 6¾ x 1 inch brownie
   pan, lightly greased and lined
   with baking parchment

MAKES 15

Preheat the oven to 170°C (325°F) Gas 3. Pour the melted chocolate into a large bowl and slowly whisk in the just-boiled water. Whisk in the sunflower oil. Beat in the muscovado sugar, and then add the cider vinegar and vanilla bean paste. Stir in the flour and baking powder.

Pour the mixture into the prepared pan, and bake for about 45 minutes, until the top of the brownie feels squidgy but set. Leave to cool in the pan, before cutting into squares. Store in an airtight tin, making sure to separate any layers with baking parchment if necessary.

LEMON YOGURT SQUARES

These luscious zingy-light lemon squares are absolute winners…BUT…I must ask nicely (but very firmly) that you resist the urge to replace the full-fat Greek yogurt with a low-fat or 0% concoction, because, without the teeniest, tiniest shred of a doubt, the recipe simply won't be the same. Baking relies on accuracy much more than any other form of cooking. The flavour and consistency of a lower fat yogurt would really spoil the recipe and would also save very little on calories.

for the base
125 g/½ cup plus 1 tablespoon
   butter, softened
200 g/1½ cups plain/all-purpose flour
50 g/¼ cup caster/superfine sugar

for the topping
500 g/1 lb. 2 oz. full-fat Greek yogurt
300 g/1½ cups caster/superfine sugar
zest of 2 lemons and juice of 4
4 eggs
2 egg yolks
80 g/⅔ cup plain/all-purpose flour

a 30 x 17 x 2.5 cm/11¾ x 6¾ x 1 inch
   brownie pan, lightly greased and lined
   with baking parchment

MAKES 15

Preheat the oven to 180°C (350°F) Gas 4.

For the base, rub the butter, flour and sugar together until the butter is evenly incorporated and the mixture resembles fine breadcrumbs. Bring the mixture together to form a ball, and press it evenly over the base of the prepared brownie pan. Transfer the pan to the oven and bake for 15 minutes, until golden and firm.

Meanwhile, for the topping, beat the yogurt, sugar and lemon zest and juice together in a large bowl. Add the eggs, egg yolks and flour, and beat together until smooth.

Remove the shortbread base from the oven and immediately pour over the yogurt mixture in an even layer. Return the pan to the oven and bake for a further 30 minutes, until the topping is set and golden. Leave to cool in the pan, and then cut into squares to serve.

APRICOT FRANGIPANE PUFF SQUARES

Sticky glazed squares of apricot-and-frangipane-topped puff pastry. Yes please. Thickly whipped fridge-cold cream is a bonus. Resistance is futile.

320 g/11½ oz. good-quality, store-bought
   puff pastry
120 g/1 stick plus 1 teaspoon
   butter, softened
150 g/¾ cup caster/superfine sugar
2 eggs
150 g/1½ cups ground almonds
650 g/23 oz. fresh apricots
   (about 16 apricots)
4 tablespoons apricot jam/jelly
   or preserves, sieved

MAKES 12

Preheat the oven to 190°C (375°F) Gas 5. Roll the pastry out to form a rectangle measuring 35 x 25 cm/14 x 9¾ inches. Lay it out on a large, flat sheet pan and turn in 1 cm/¾ inch along each side towards the centre.

Beat the butter and sugar together in a large bowl and add the eggs. Beat until well mixed. Add the ground almonds and beat again, until the mixture is smooth. Spoon it onto the pastry, and spread it in an even layer with a spatula. Cut the apricots in half and remove the pits. Arrange them (quite closely together) over the frangipane mixture. Transfer the sheet pan to the oven and bake for about 35–40 minutes, until the frangipane is firm and the apricots are softened and a little charred here and there. Remove from the oven and brush with the sieved jam/jelly. Cut into squares and serve warm or cold, with thickly whipped cream or ice cream.

COCONUT MACAROON QUEEN OF PUDDINGS

200 g/7 oz. desiccated/dried
 shredded coconut
80 g/⅓ cup plus 1 teaspoon butter
50 g/¼ cup caster/superfine sugar
1 teaspoon vanilla bean paste
2 eggs, plus 1 egg yolk
300 g/10½ oz. raspberry or strawberry
 jam/jelly
3 egg whites
150 g/¾ cup caster/superfine sugar

a 30 x 17 x 2.5 cm/11¾ x 6¾ x 1 inch
 brownie pan, lightly greased and lined
 with baking parchment

SERVES 4-6

Queen of puddings is an old-fashioned British nursery pudding made of bread or cake crumbs cooked in an egg custard, topped with jam/jelly and crowned with meringue. I've swapped the traditional base for a chewy coconut macaroon mixture, which I think adds something deliciously different and rather special.

Preheat the oven to 170°C (325°F) Gas 3. Rub the coconut and butter together in a bowl until the butter has been evenly incorporated. Add the 50 g/¼ cup of sugar, the vanilla bean paste, eggs and egg yolk. Stir to combine. Spoon the mixture evenly into the prepared brownie pan and smooth over with a palette knife. Bake for 20 minutes, until golden and firm.

Spread the jam/jelly evenly over the coconut base.

Whisk the egg whites until firm and glossy. Gradually add the 150 g/¾ cup of sugar, whisking a little after each addition, until the sugar has been fully incorporated and the meringue is glossy and firm. Pipe or spoon it over the jam/jelly. Return the brownie pan to the oven and bake for a further 20–25 minutes, until the meringue is golden brown and crisp. Serve warm or cold.

CHERRY, WHITE CHOCOLATE & RATAFIA BRIOCHE & BUTTER PUDDING

300 g/10½ oz. brioche
50 g/3½ tablespoons butter, softened
250 g/9 oz. cherries, pitted
75 g/2¾ oz. white chocolate,
 roughly chopped
4 eggs
250 ml/1 cup plus 1 tablespoon double/
 heavy cream
150 ml/⅔ cup whole milk
1 teaspoon vanilla bean paste
50 g/1¾ oz. ratafia biscuits or crisp
 amaretti biscuits, crumbled
cream or ice cream, to serve

a 30 x 17 x 2.5 cm/11¾ x 6¾ x 1 inch
 brownie pan, lightly greased and lined
 with baking parchment

SERVES 4-6

Speckled with juicy cherries and little nuggets of creamy white chocolate, this dreamy, crunchy-topped pudding is awesome. Dangerously so. But you're worth it, and so are the people you'll be sharing it with.

Preheat the oven to 170°C (325°F) Gas 3. Cut the brioche into 1 cm/⅜ inch slices (no need to cut the crusts off), butter them on one side, and then cut each slice into quarters, diagonally. Arrange the brioche triangles across the base of the prepared brownie pan, standing them up slightly. Scatter the cherries and the chopped white chocolate evenly over the top, and then push some of the cherries into the brioche here and there.

Beat the eggs, double/heavy cream, milk and vanilla bean paste together in a large bowl. Pour the mixture through a fine sieve, over the brioche and fruit.

Scatter the crumbled ratafia or amaretti biscuits evenly over the top of the pudding, and transfer to the oven. Bake for about 30 minutes, until the custard is lightly set and the topping is crisp and golden. Serve warm, with extra cream or ice cream.

INDEX

almonds: apricot frangipane puff
squares 170
chickpea & almond curry 114
roasted red pepper, chilli &
almond dip 156
white chocolate, almond &
raspberry ripple brownies 169
apples: apple & blackberry almond
crumble 165
duck legs with apple, parsnip &
white cabbage 56
apricot frangipane puff squares
170
asparagus: chicken nuggets with
asparagus 47
tamari & ginger salmon with
asparagus 70
avocados: avocado hollandaise
130
avocado spread 129
crushed butter beans with
roasted tomatoes & avocado
105
guacamole 51
harissa-baked avocado, butternut
squash & eggs 85

bakes: grain-free tomato 'spaghetti'
94
Greek potato & courgette 101
harissa chicken & chickpea 44
honey & mustard sausage 17
honey harissa halloumi 93
Mexican vegetable & kidney bean
130
pesto summer veg 109
sausage, celery & tomato 18
Spanish red pepper & chicken
44
Thai salmon 61
white fish & chorizo 66
bananas: baked chocolate bananas
162
banana butter flapjacks 162
beans: marinated lamb chops with
garlicky tomatoes & white
beans 34
ratatouille baked beans 126
roast chicken & beans 52
see also individual types of
beans
beef: beef & chorizo meatballs 22
beef-stuffed tomatoes 29
crowd-pleaser meatloaf 21
root veg & corned beef hash 22
spicy roast beef 26
steak & chips 29
steak burgers 25
beetroot: salt-baked heritage
beetroot & mango lettuce cups
151
black beans: black bean & sweet
potato chilli 126
black bean & sweetcorn hash 77

black bean nachos 86
black-eyed beans: roasted pepper,
sweetcorn & black-eyed bean
wraps 129
blackberries: apple & blackberry
almond crumble 165
bread: crispy baguette croutons
82
leek, red pepper & brie strata 81
pappa al pomodoro 82
breakfast, all-in-one 13
breakfast slice 13
brioche: cherry, white chocolate &
ratafia brioche & butter pudding
173
broccoli: garlic broccoli 21, 25
purple sprouting broccoli &
flageolet beans 78
roasted red cabbage with
charred broccoli, cherries &
almonds 78
brownies: vegan brownies 169
white chocolate, almond &
raspberry ripple brownies 169
burgers: minty lamb burgers 30
roasted Roquefort burgers 25
steak burgers 25
butter beans: crushed butter beans
with roasted tomatoes & avocado
105

cabbage: duck legs with apple,
parsnip & white cabbage 56
roasted red cabbage with
charred broccoli, cherries &
almonds 78
spicy roast beef with butternut
squash & cabbage 26
Cajun salmon 69
cakes: lemon yogurt squares 170
sticky ginger cake 166
vegan brownies 169
white chocolate, almond &
raspberry ripple brownies 169
carrots: 7-hour lamb with roasted
carrots & celeriac 37
carrot tart tatin squares 98
garlic roasted chicken with
shallots & carrots 55
smoky lamb ribs with slow-
roasted carrots 30
cauliflower: balsamic tempeh &
crispy cauliflower 122
butternut squash & cauliflower
lentil korma 118
cauliflower, sultana & mango
salad 148
Indian prawns with cauliflower 70
saffron cauliflower steaks 113
celeriac: 7-hour lamb with roasted
carrots & celeriac 37
celeriac, sultana & caper salad
155
celery: sausage, celery & tomato
bake 18
cheese: baked honey & thyme
Camembert 89

baked Mediterranean feta 89
courgette & sun-dried tomato
fritters 147
fondant tomatoes with basil &
burrata 140
goats' cheese & veg stacks 90
grain-free tomato 'spaghetti'
bake with Roquefort 94
Greek potato & courgette bake
101
honey harissa halloumi bake 93
leek, red pepper & brie strata 81
pan haggerty 136
parsnips Molly Parkin 139
roast mini peppers with feta,
olives & pesto 98
roasted Roquefort burgers 25
slow-baked onions with goats'
cheese 82
spiced tomatoes with paneer &
peas 148
twice-baked cheesy potatoes
135
warm halloumi, fig & pistachio
salad 147
chermoula, lime 113
cherries: cherry, white chocolate &
ratafia brioche & butter
pudding 173
roasted red cabbage with
charred broccoli, cherries &
almonds 78
chicken: cheat's chicken Kiev 48
chicken fajitas 51
chicken nuggets 47
coq au vin 43
cornflake chicken nuggets 47
garlic roasted chicken 55
harissa chicken & chickpea bake
44
Moroccan chicken 52
roast chicken & beans 52
roasted chicken thighs with
plums & tarragon 48
Spanish red pepper & chicken
bake 44
chickpeas: chickpea & almond
curry 114
harissa chicken & chickpea bake
44
vegan baked fajitas 121
chillies: black bean & sweet potato
chilli 126
oven-roasted chilli jam 156
roasted red pepper, chilli &
almond dip 156
chips, steak & 29
chocolate: baked chocolate
bananas 162
cherry, white chocolate & ratafia
brioche & butter pudding 173
vegan brownies 169
white chocolate, almond &
raspberry ripple brownies 169
chorizo: baked eggs with chorizo,
tomato & spinach 14
beef & chorizo meatballs 22

white fish & chorizo bake 66
clafoutis, baby plum tomato 140
coconut: coconut macaroon queen
of puddings 173
grain-free granola 161
coconut milk: fresh lime, vegetable
& coconut curry 117
cod: cod baked in tomato & olive
sauce 65
cod loin with balsamic fennel 65
coq au vin 43
corned beef: root veg & corned
beef hash 22
cornflake chicken nuggets 47
courgettes/zucchini: breakfast slice
13
cheat's chicken Kiev with
courgettes 48
courgette & sun-dried tomato
fritters 147
courgette crust mini pesto
quiches 90
grain-free tomato 'spaghetti'
bake 94
Greek potato & courgette bake
101
sweet potato falafel 110
crumble, apple & blackberry
almond 165
curry: butternut squash &
cauliflower lentil korma 118
chickpea & almond curry 114
fresh lime, vegetable & coconut
curry 117
Indian prawns with cauliflower 70

dal, easy oven 114
dip, roasted red pepper, chilli &
almond 156
duck: duck in orange glaze 56
duck legs with apple, parsnip &
white cabbage 56

eggs: all-in-one breakfast 13
baked eggs with chorizo, tomato
& spinach 14
baked frittata 86
breakfast slice 13
cherry tomato, roasted pepper &
spinach Bombay eggs 81
harissa-baked avocado, butternut
squash & eggs 85
sweet potato & kale hash with
baked eggs 14

fajitas: chicken fajitas 51
vegan baked fajitas 121
falafels, sweet potato 110
fennel, cod loin with balsamic 65
figs: roasted fig salad 93
warm halloumi, fig & pistachio
salad 147
fish 58–73
Mediterranean baked fish fillets
62
white fish & chorizo bake 66
see also cod; salmon, etc

flageolet beans, purple sprouting broccoli & 78
flapjacks, banana butter 162
frangipane puff squares, apricot 170
frittata, baked 86
fritters, courgette & sun-dried tomato 147

garlic: garlic broccoli 21, 25
garlic roasted chicken 55
marinated lamb chops with garlicky tomatoes 34
ginger: sticky ginger cake 166
tamari & ginger salmon 70
granola, grain-free 161
Greek potato & courgette bake 101
guacamole 51

halibut, tomato pesto 62
halloumi: honey harissa halloumi bake 93
warm halloumi, fig & pistachio salad 147
harissa: harissa-baked avocado, butternut squash & eggs 85
harissa chicken & chickpea bake 44
honey harissa halloumi bake 93
hash: black bean & sweetcorn hash 77
root veg & corned beef hash 22
sweet potato & kale hash 14
hollandaise, avocado 130
honey: baked honey & thyme Camembert 89
honey & mustard sausage bake 17
honey harissa halloumi bake 93
honey mustard lamb 38

Indian prawns with cauliflower 70

jam, oven-roasted chilli 156
jerk pineapple pork loin 18
jerk veggie skewers 155
Jerusalem artichokes, saffron cauliflower steaks with candied 113

kale: sweet potato & kale hash 14
kidney beans: Mexican vegetable & kidney bean bake 130
Kiev, cheat's chicken 48
korma, butternut squash & cauliflower lentil 118

lamb: 7-hour lamb 37
honey mustard lamb 38
lamb kofta meatballs 33
lamb skewers 33
marinated lamb chops with garlicky tomatoes & white beans 34
minty lamb burgers 30
perfect roast lamb chops 34

smoky lamb ribs 30
leeks: Cajun salmon with crispy leeks & butternut squash 69
duck in orange glaze on a bed of leeks & mushrooms 56
leek, red pepper & brie strata 81
lemons: lemon & butter baked salmon 66
lemon yogurt squares 170
lentils: butternut squash & cauliflower lentil korma 118
cauliflower, sultana & mango salad with lentils 148
easy oven dal 114
roast butternut squash with black beluga lentils 139
lettuce: salt-baked heritage beetroot & mango lettuce cups 151
lime: fresh lime, vegetable & coconut curry 117

macadamias, turmeric 117
macaroon queen of puddings, coconut 173
mangos: cauliflower, sultana & mango salad 148
salt-baked heritage beetroot & mango lettuce cups 151
meatballs: beef & chorizo meatballs 22
lamb kofta meatballs 33
pork meatballs 17
meatloaf, crowd-pleaser 21
Mediterranean baked fish fillets 62
Mediterranean sauce 22
Mexican vegetable & kidney bean bake 130
mole-style mushrooms 129
monkfish: roasted monkfish & Parma ham parcels 73
Moroccan chicken 52
muffins, smoked salmon 61
mushrooms: duck in orange glaze on a bed of leeks & mushrooms 56
mole-style mushrooms 129
pesto-baked mushrooms 106

nachos, black bean 86

oats: banana butter flapjacks 162
olives: chicken nuggets with roasted tomatoes, olives & asparagus 47
cod baked in tomato & olive sauce 65
roast mini peppers with feta, olives & pesto 98
onions: charred turnip, radish & red onion salad 144
slow-baked onions with goats' cheese 82
orange-baked rhubarb 165

pan haggerty 136
paneer: spiced tomatoes with

paneer & peas 148
pappa al pomodoro 82
Parma ham: all-in-one breakfast 13
roasted monkfish & Parma ham parcels 73
parsnips: duck legs with apple, parsnip & white cabbage 56
honey mustard lamb & parsnips 38
parsnips Molly Parkin 139
peas, spiced tomatoes with paneer & 148
pelau, Trinidadian vegetable 155
peppers: beef & chorizo meatballs 22
cherry tomato, roasted pepper & spinach Bombay eggs 81
leek, red pepper & brie strata 81
roast mini peppers with feta, olives & pesto 98
roasted pepper, sweetcorn & black-eyed bean wraps 129
roasted red pepper, chilli & almond dip 156
Spanish red pepper & chicken bake 44
sweet potato falafel with courgettes & peppers 110
pesto: courgette crust mini pesto quiches 90
pesto-baked mushrooms 106
pesto summer veg bake 109
roast mini peppers with feta, olives & pesto 98
tomato pesto halibut 62
vegan pesto 106
pineapple: jerk pineapple pork loin 18
roasted pineapple 161
pistachios: warm halloumi, fig & pistachio salad 147
pizza, potato & rosemary 97
plums, roasted chicken thighs with 48
pork: jerk pineapple pork loin 18
pork meatballs 17
potatoes: crispy Bengali 5 spice potatoes 152
dill potatoes 73
pan haggerty 136
potato & rosemary pizza 97
roast potatoes 48, 70, 135
rosemary & thyme Anna potatoes 136
twice-baked cheesy potatoes 135
prawns, Indian 70
puff squares, apricot frangipane 170
purple sprouting broccoli & flageolet beans 78

queen of puddings, coconut macaroon 173
quiches, courgette crust mini pesto 90

radishes: charred turnip, radish & red onion salad 144
raita, coriander 152
raspberries: white chocolate, almond & raspberry ripple brownies 169
ratafia biscuits: cherry, white chocolate & ratafia brioche & butter pudding 173
ratatouille baked beans 126
rhubarb, orange-baked 165
rice: crispy rice with soy & ginger tempeh 70
oven-baked butternut squash, saffron & rosemary risotto 97
Trinidadian vegetable pelau 155
vegetable risotto 109
risotto: oven-baked butternut squash, saffron & rosemary risotto 97
vegetable risotto 109

salads: cauliflower, sultana & mango salad 148
celeriac, sultana & caper salad 155
charred turnip, radish & red onion salad 144
roasted fig salad 93
warm halloumi, fig & pistachio salad 147
salmon: Cajun salmon 69
lemon & butter baked salmon 66
smoked salmon muffins 61
tamari & ginger salmon 70
Thai salmon bake 61
sausages: honey & mustard sausage bake 17
sausage, celery & tomato bake 18
skewers: jerk veggie skewers 155
lamb skewers 33
Spanish red pepper & chicken bake 44
spicy roast beef 26
spinach: baked eggs with chorizo, tomato & spinach 14
cherry tomato, roasted pepper & spinach Bombay eggs 81
sprouts, pork meatballs with 17
squash: butternut squash & cauliflower lentil korma 118
Cajun salmon with crispy leeks & butternut squash 69
harissa-baked avocado, butternut squash & eggs 85
hasselback coquina squash 125
oven-baked butternut squash, saffron & rosemary risotto 97
roast butternut squash with black beluga lentils 139
spicy roast beef with butternut squash & cabbage 26
sticky ginger cake 166
sultanas: celeriac, sultana & caper salad 155
sultana & mango salad with

lentils 148
sweet potatoes: baked sweet
    potatoes with miso butter 151
black bean & sweet potato chilli
    126
fragrant sweet potato wedges
    33
pork meatballs with sprouts &
    sweet potato 17
sweet potato & kale hash 14
sweet potato chips 29, 47
sweet potato falafel 110
tamarind & rosemary sweet
    potatoes 144
sweetcorn: black bean &
    sweetcorn hash 77
roasted pepper, sweetcorn &
    black-eyed bean wraps 129

tamari & ginger salmon 70
tart tatin, carrots 98
tempeh: balsamic tempeh & crispy
    cauliflower 122
crispy rice with soy & ginger
    tempeh 152
Thai salmon bake 61
tian, bay-scented summer

vegetable 101
tofu: turmeric tofu & roasted veggie
    scramble 105
tomatoes: baby plum tomato
    clafoutis 140
baked eggs with chorizo, tomato
    & spinach 14
beef-stuffed tomatoes 29
cheat's chicken Kiev with
    tomatoes 48
cherry tomato, roasted pepper &
    spinach Bombay eggs 81
chicken nuggets with roasted
    tomatoes 47
cod baked in tomato & olive
    sauce 65
cornflake chicken nuggets with
    roasted cherry tomatoes 47
courgette & sun-dried tomato
    fritters 147
crushed butter beans with
    roasted tomatoes 105
easy oven dal 114
fondant tomatoes with basil &
    burrata 140
grain-free tomato 'spaghetti'
    bake 94

marinated lamb chops with
    garlicky tomatoes 34
pappa al pomodoro 82
parsnips Molly Parkin 139
pesto-baked mushrooms with
    sun-dried tomatoes 106
sausage, celery & tomato bake
    18
spiced tomatoes with paneer &
    peas 148
tomato pesto halibut 62
Trinidadian vegetable pelau 155
turnips: charred turnip, radish & red
    onion salad 144

vegetables: bay-scented summer
    vegetable tian 101
fresh lime, vegetable & coconut
    curry 117
goats' cheese & veg stacks 90
jerk veggie skewers 155
lamb skewers with roasted veg
    33
lemon & butter baked salmon
    with spring vegetables 66
Mexican vegetable & kidney bean
    bake 130

minty lamb burgers & veg 30
perfect roast lamb chops with
    rosemary vegetables 34
pesto summer veg bake 109
roast chicken & beans with root
    vegetables 52
roasted Mediterranean
    vegetables 143
root veg & corned beef hash 22
steak burgers with balsamic
    roast vegetables 25
tomato pesto halibut with green
    veg 62
Trinidadian vegetable pelau 155
turmeric tofu & roasted veggie
    scramble 105
vegetable risotto 109

wine: coq au vin 43
wraps, roasted pepper, sweetcorn
    & black-eyed bean 129

yogurt: lemon yogurt squares 170

RECIPE CREDITS

All recipes by Jenny Tschiesche with the exception of the following, by Liz Franklin:

Cherry roasted pepper & spinach Bombay eggs
Leek, red pepper & brie strata
Purple sprouting broccoli with flageolet beans & preserved lemon mayo
Roasted red cabbage with charred broccoli, cherries & almonds
Slow-baked onions with goats' cheese, crispy baguette croutons,
    walnuts & balsamic dressing
Pappa al pomodoro
Potato & rosemary pizza
Baked butternut squash, saffron & rosemary risotto
Carrot tart Tatin squares with ginger & mint yogurt
Roasted mini peppers with feta, olives & pesto
Greek potato & courgette bake with feta & fresh herbs
Bay-scented summer vegetable tian
Crushed butter beans with roasted tomatoes & avocado
Turmeric tofu & roasted veggie scramble
Crushed butter beans with roasted tomatoes & avocado
Turmeric tofu & roasted veggie scramble
Saffron cauliflower steaks with candied Jerusalem artichokes,
    roasted grapes, pistachios & lime chermoula
Fresh lime, vegetable & coconut curry
Turmeric macadamias
Chickpea & almond curry
Easy oven dal
Hasselback coquina squash with chilli maple glaze & salt flakes
Mexican vegetable & kidney bean bake with avocado hollandaise
Roasted pepper, sweetcorn & black eyed-bean wraps with
    chipotle dressing & avocado spread
Mole-style mushrooms
Pan haggerty

Rosemary & thyme anna potatoes
Roast butternut squash with black beluga lentils, pomegranates
    & pine nuts
Parsnips Molly Parkin
Roasted Mediterranean vegetables with balsamic dressing
Fondant tomatoes with basil & burrata
Baby plum tomato clafoutis
Courgette & sun-dried tomato fritters with sumac kefalotyri
Warm halloumi, fig & pistachio salad
Charred turnip, radish & red onion salad
Tamarind & rosemary sweet potatoes
Cauliflower, sultana & mango salad with lentils & turmeric, ginger
    & maple dressing
Spiced tomatoes with paneer & peas
Salt-baked heritage beetroot & mango lettuce cups with nerigoma
    dressing
Baked sweet potatoes with miso butter, chives & black sesame
Crispy Bengali five spice potatoes with spring onions & chilli
    & coriander raita
Crispy rice with soy & ginger tempeh
Jerk veggie skewers with celeriac, sultana & caper salad
Trinidadian vegetable pilau
Oven-roasted chilli jam
Roasted red pepper, chilli & almond dip with tortilla crisps
White chocolate, almond & raspberry ripple brownies
Vegan brownies
Leman yogurt squares
Apricot frangipane puff squares
Coconut macaroon queen of puddings
Cherry, white chocolate & ratafia brioche & butter pudding